Sabrina

BY NICK DRNASO

GRANTA.COM
GRANTA PUBLICATIONS, 12 ADDISON AVENUE, LONDON W11 4QR

FIRST PUBLISHED IN GREAT BRITAIN BY GRANTA BOOKS, 2018

PUBLISHED BY ARRANGEMENT WITH TRANSATLANTIC LITERARY AGENCY INC. AND DRAWN & QUARTERY, A CLIENT PUBLISHER OF FARRAR, STRAUS & GIROUX, NEW YORK, USA.
DRAWNANDQUARTERLY.COM

A CIP CATALOGUE RECORD FOR THIS BOOK IS AVAILABLE FROM THE BRITISH LIBRARY.

3 5 7 9 10 8 6 4 2

ISBN 978 1 78378 490 5

PRINTED IN ITALY

THANKS: KYLE HORTON, IVAN BRUNETTI, TRACY HURREN, CHRIS OLIVEROS, CHRISTEN CARTER, MICHELLE OLLIE, HARRY BLISS, JAMES STURM, SUSAN O'DELL, ZADIE SMITH, TONY TULATHIMUTTE, ADRIAN TOMINE, JONATHAN LETHEM, CHRIS WARE, PEGGY BURNS, TOM DEVLIN, JULIA POHL-MIRANDA, RACHEL NAM.

♥ FOR SARAH. ♥

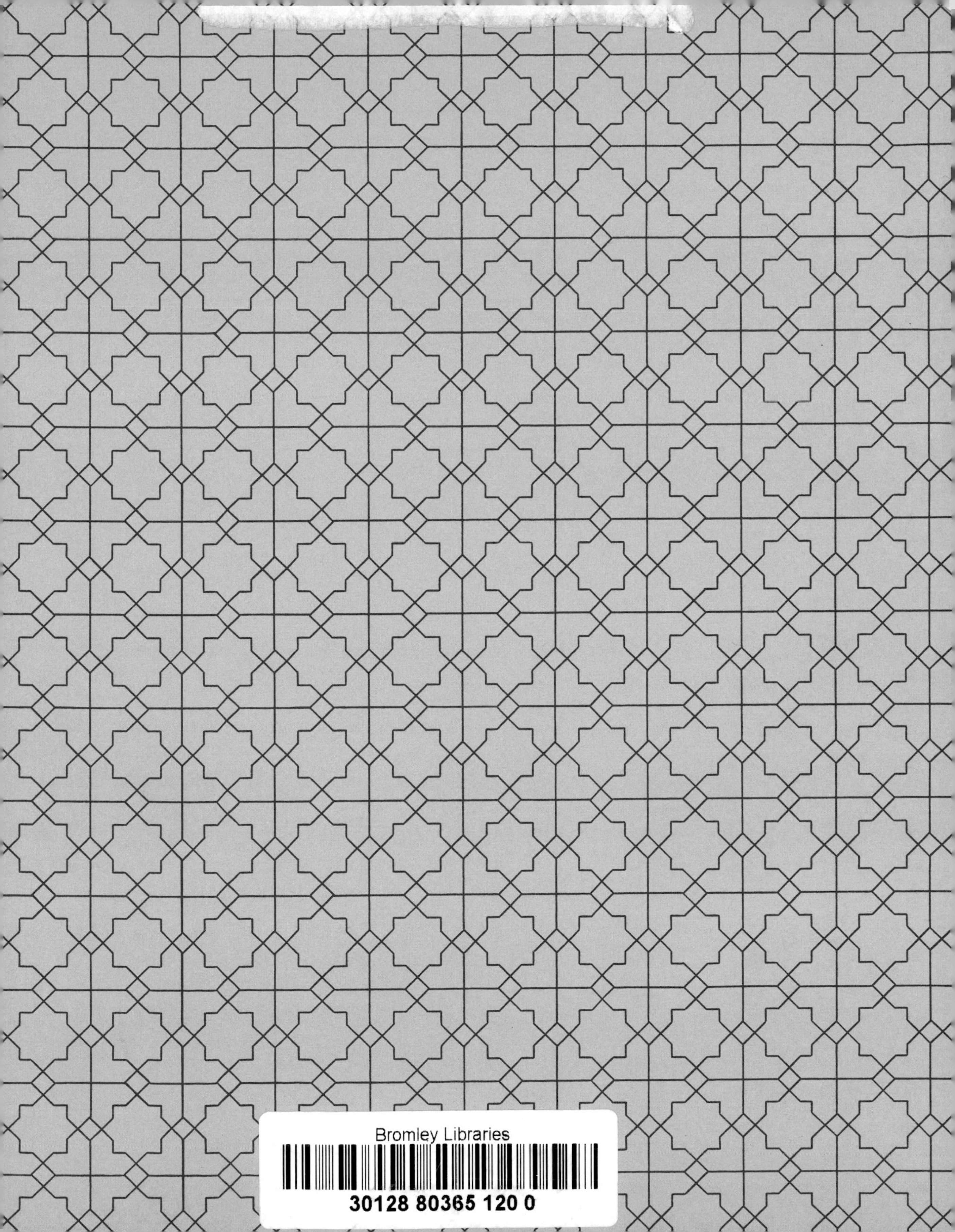
Bromley Libraries
30128 80365 120 0

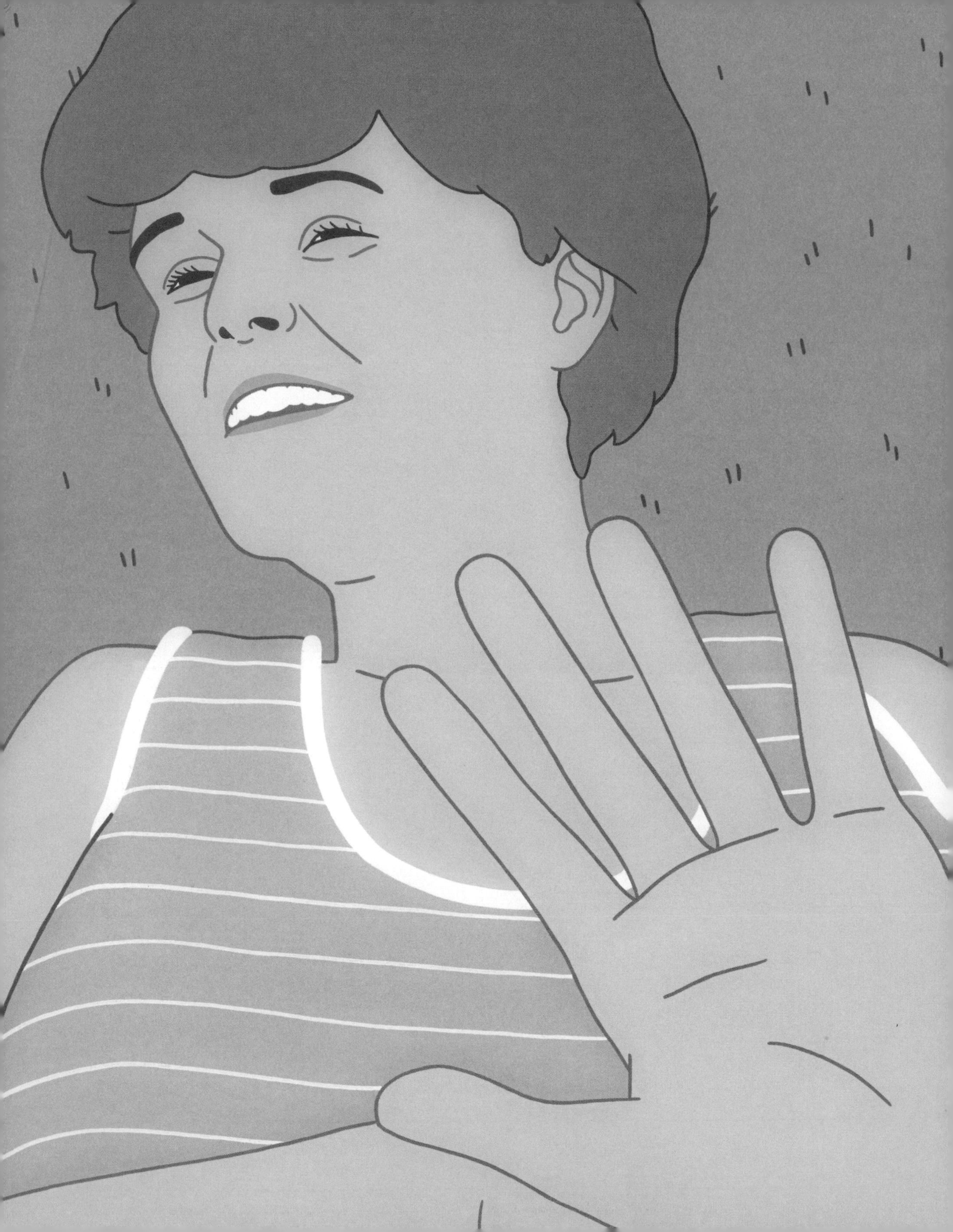

THERE YOU ARE!
WHY WERE YOU HIDING FROM ME?
LOOK AT THAT FACE.
DO YOU WANT SUPPER?
GOD!
DON'T DO THAT!
SORRY!
I TOLD YOU I WAS COMING OVER AFTER WORK.
IT'S ALL RIGHT. I GUESS I'M NOT USED TO BEING ALONE AT NIGHT.

HOW'S THE FAT LADY?

SHE LOOKS SO OLD, DOESN'T SHE?

YEA, BUT DON'T SAY THAT TO MOM. SHE'S GONNA LOSE HER MIND WHEN THAT CAT DIES.

HM.

WHERE'S YOUR MAN?

HE HAD TO WORK. I THOUGHT IT WOULD BE WEIRD TO SPEND THE NIGHT WITH HIM IN MY OLD BED-ROOM ANYWAY.

BUT YOU COULD HAVE DONE FAN-TASY ROLE-PLAYING! PARENTS ARE OUT OF TOWN... HOME ALONE WITH YOUR BOYFRIEND...

DON'T BE BOORISH, SANDRA.

HEY, WOULD YOU RUB MY SHOULDER FOR A MINUTE? THIS JOB IS KILLING ME.

HOW'S THAT?

SO GOOD.

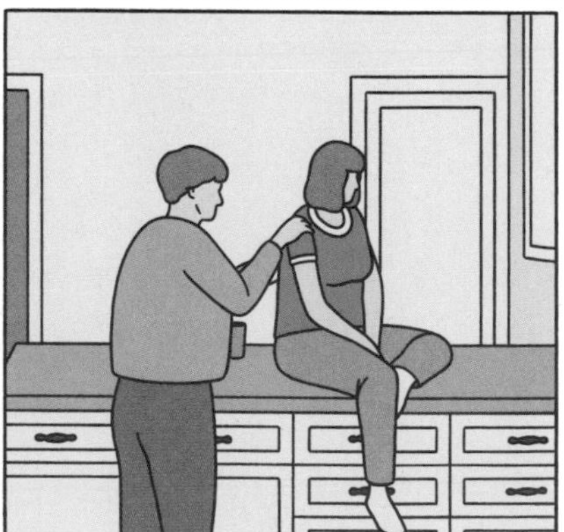

MOM USED TO RUB MY SHOULDERS WHILE I STUDIED.
LAST YEAR WHEN I WAS REALLY FREAKING OUT, I CAME OVER HERE AND SHE SCRATCHED MY BACK.
DO YOU HAVE MY BOOK?
YEA! THANKS FOR REMINDING ME.
WHAT DID YOU THINK?
THERE WERE SOME INTERESTING IDEAS, BUT I FELT EMPTY WHEN IT WAS OVER.
YEA. IT WAS A GOOD KIND OF EMPTY FEELING THOUGH. DID TEDDY READ IT?
OH, NO. HE'S NOT MUCH OF A READER.
REALLY?
HE HAS A LOT OF OTHER INTERESTS. I DID GIVE HIM THIS WEIRD, OLD BOOK ABOUT PIRATES FOR CHRISTMAS THAT I THINK HE LIKED.
I FORGOT THESE WERE FAKE.
I REPAINTED THEM. DON'T THEY LOOK REAL?

WHEN DO MOM AND DAD COME HOME?

MONDAY. ARE YOU STILL GOING TO THAT SURPRISE PARTY TONIGHT?

YEA, I'M SORRY I CAN'T STAY LONG. WOULDN'T WANT TO SHOW UP LATE AND RUIN THE SURPRISE. I HATE THESE STUPID GATHERINGS.

DO YOU WANT TO SKIP IT? WE COULD ORDER PIZZA AND HAVE A GIRLS' NIGHT.

NAH, I CAN'T GET OUT OF IT.

WANNA HELP ME WITH THIS CROSS-WORD PUZZLE?

TWELVE LETTERS. WE KILLED THE CLUTTER FAMILY.

DICK AND PERRY.

I KNEW THAT.

ARE YOU STILL LOOKING FOR A NEW JOB?

YEA. I HAD AN INTERVIEW LAST WEEK FOR A SALES JOB THAT TURNED OUT TO BE VACUUM SALES, DOOR-TO-DOOR.

THE BUSINESS WAS RUN OUT OF THIS WEIRD GUY'S APARTMENT. HE WAS WEARING THIS PINK, FUZZY SWEATER AND AN EXPEN-SIVE WATCH. IT MUST HAVE BEEN SOME KIND OF SCAM.

YOU KNOW, WHEN I WAS IN THE HOSPITAL, THERE WERE PEOPLE STAYING THERE AS PART OF A MED-ICAL STUDY. THEY WERE CONFINED THERE AS PATIENTS WITH US FOR AN ENTIRE MONTH AND PAID TWO-THOUSAND DOLLARS.

HA, I DON'T KNOW IF I'M THAT DESPERATE. I WOULDN'T LIKE BEING TRAPPED IN THERE.

IT'S NOT THAT BAD, JUST KIND OF BORING. WE WOULD WATCH THE SAME VHS TAPES OVER AND OVER. I STARTED STUDYING THE ACTORS IN THE BACKGROUND BECAUSE THERE WAS NOTHING ELSE TO DO.

HM.

YOU WOULD MEET INTERESTING PEOPLE, THAT'S FOR SURE. I BET YOU WOULD GET SOME GOOD STORIES OUT OF IT.

YEA, HA HA, MAYBE. I WAS THINKING ABOUT SOMETHING MORE LIKE DOG WALKING.

WHO SANG "STAND BY YOUR MAN?"

WHAT? OH-
TAMMY WYNETTE.

HEY, YOU KNOW STUFF! YOU SHOULD JUST GO ON A GAME SHOW AND WIN A PILE OF MONEY.

THAT'S AN IDEA.

I MIGHT GO ON A BIKE RIDE AROUND THE GREAT LAKES THIS SPRING.

YOU SHOULD! THAT WOULD BE AMAZING.

OUR COUSIN GINA TOLD ME ABOUT A PATH SHE RODE LAST YEAR THAT'S TOTALLY BEAUTIFUL.

THAT SOUNDS GREAT. GET OUT OF THE CITY. GET AWAY FROM THE INTERNET.

MAYBE YOU WOULD WANNA COME WITH ME?

REALLY? WHERE WOULD WE STAY?

WE CAN JUST PITCH A TENT OFF THE PATH. IT WOULDN'T COST A THING IF THAT'S WHAT YOU'RE WORRIED ABOUT.

IS IT SAFE?

I HAVE NO IDEA. WHAT COULD HAPPEN?

I DON'T KNOW. FALLING OFF A CLIFF. WILD ANIMALS.

REMEMBER WHEN I WAS NINE-TEEN AND I RODE A BUS TO PANAMA CITY BEACH BY MYSELF?

YEA. WHAT COMPELLED YOU TO DO THAT?

I JUST WANTED TO DO IT. I DON'T KNOW WHAT I EXPECTED TO GET OUT OF IT.

I WAS THROWN INTO A SPRING BREAK NIGHTMARE. IT WAS TER-RIFYING. THE PLACE WAS LOUSY WITH COLLEGE DATE RAPISTS AND STEROID FREAKS.

I HAD JUST ENOUGH MONEY TO STAY IN THE WORST MOTEL OFF THE MAIN STRIP. I CALLED MOM ON THE FIRST NIGHT AND SHE DIDN'T EVEN REALIZE I HAD LEFT CHICAGO.

I DIDN'T HAVE ANYTHING TO DO DURING THE DAY SO I SAT IN THIS OLD ARCADE AND WATCHED PEOPLE PLAY AIR HOCKEY. AT NIGHT, I HID IN MY ROOM AND WATCHED PUBLIC-ACCESS.

I WAS WATCHING THE SUNSET ON THE BEACH MY LAST NIGHT, AND THESE THREE GUYS WALKED UP AND ASKED ME BACK TO THEIR ROOM. ONE OF THEM SAID THEY WERE OUT HUNTING.

I STARTED WALKING AWAY AND HE GRABBED MY ARM. I RAN TO THE STREET AND THEY GOT IN THEIR CAR AND STARTED FOLLOWING ME. I DUCKED INTO THIS TACO PLACE AND HID IN THE BATHROOM FOR TWO HOURS, CRYING.

YOU NEVER TOLD ME THAT.

I WAS TOO PROUD. YOU KNOW, I HAVEN'T BEEN ON VACATION SINCE.

SO ANYWAY, DON'T WORRY ABOUT RIDING A BIKE THROUGH THE WOODS. THE FUCKING WILD ANIMALS STAY IN HOTELS.

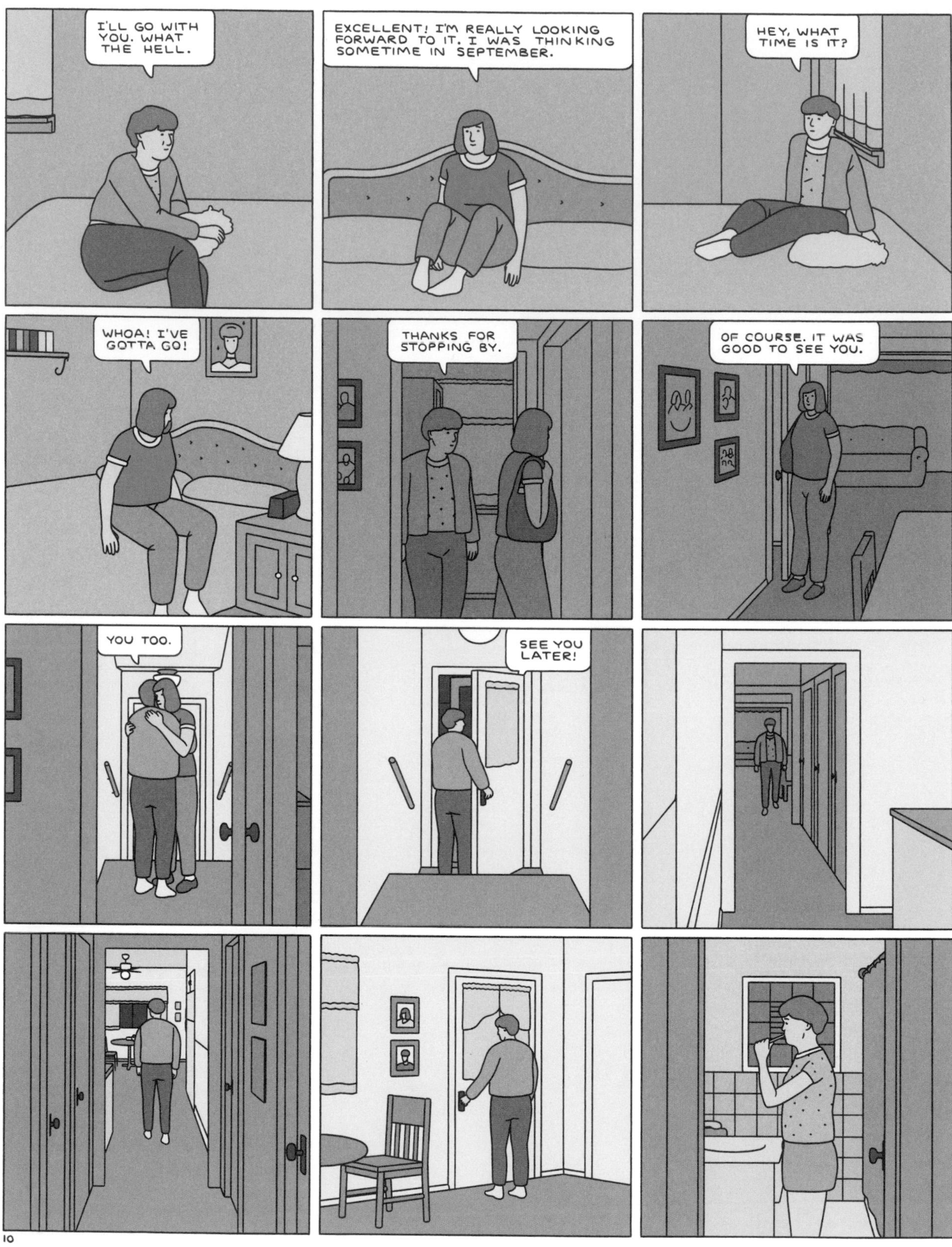
I'LL GO WITH YOU. WHAT THE HELL.
EXCELLENT! I'M REALLY LOOKING FORWARD TO IT. I WAS THINKING SOMETIME IN SEPTEMBER.
HEY, WHAT TIME IS IT?
WHOA! I'VE GOTTA GO!
THANKS FOR STOPPING BY.
OF COURSE. IT WAS GOOD TO SEE YOU.
YOU TOO.
SEE YOU LATER!

Gate F

TEDDY.
HEY, MAN.
HEY, CALVIN.
HOW WAS THE TRAIN?
IT WAS GOOD.
YEA...
I LIKE YOUR HAIR.
WELL...
I'M PARKED OUT FRONT IF YOU'RE READY.

ARE YOU HUNGRY?
I CAN STOP SOMEWHERE IF YOU'D LIKE.
NO, THANKS.
I KNOW THE CIRCUM-STANCES ARE AWFUL, BUT IT'S STILL GOOD TO SEE YOU.
I'M GLAD YOU STILL FELT LIKE YOU COULD REACH OUT TO ME.
YEA.
IT WILL BE NICE TO HAVE SOME COMPANY AT THE HOUSE.
HM.

THAT'S CHEYENNE MOUNTAIN.

THAT'S WHERE THEY BUILT THE NORAD COMPLEX IN THE SIXTIES.

THERE'S A BUNKER DEEP UNDER THERE WITH A CAFETERIA, CONVENIENCE STORE, GYM, AND CHAPEL THAT CAN WITHSTAND A FULL-BLOWN NUCLEAR ATTACK. PRETTY WEIRD, RIGHT?

HM.

DO YOU REMEMBER THIS SONG?

PLAY

YOU MADE ME THIS MIX FOR MY TWELFTH BIRTHDAY. I PULLED IT OUT WHEN I KNEW YOU WERE COMING.

WHOOPS. I'M SORRY, MAN. WE DON'T HAVE TO LISTEN TO IT.

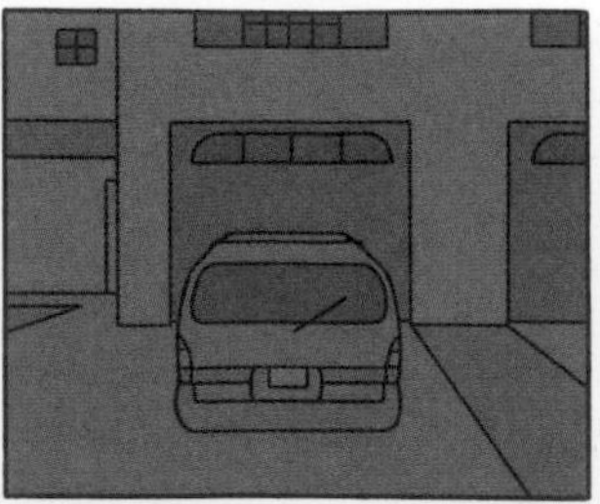

HOME SWEET HOME.

HI, RANDY. COME HERE.

RANDY, THIS IS TEDDY. HE'S GONNA BE STAYING WITH US FOR A WHILE.

YOU DIDN'T BRING ANY LUGGAGE.

LET ME GIVE YOU A TOUR OF THE HOUSE.

YEA. I GUESS I FORGOT.

WELL, YOU'RE WELCOME TO TAKE ANYTHING YOU NEED. SERIOUSLY, DON'T EVEN ASK. WE CAN GO OUT THIS WEEKEND AND PICK UP SOME STUFF.

I'M SORRY, I DON'T REALLY KEEP FOOD IN THE HOUSE.

WE'LL STOCK UP ON WHATEVER YOU NEED AT THE STORE.

MAKE YOURSELF AT HOME. WATCH TV, WHATEVER YOU WANT.

THIS COUCH IS PRETTY COMFORTABLE IF YOU EVER WANT TO SLEEP DOWN HERE.

WHAT ELSE... I THINK THAT'S IT.

LET'S GO UPSTAIRS.

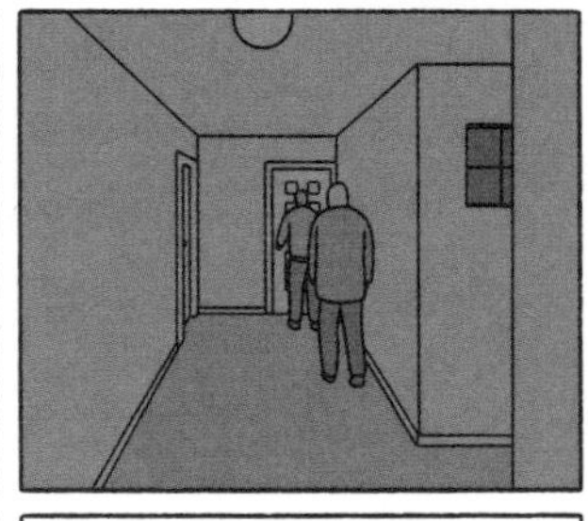

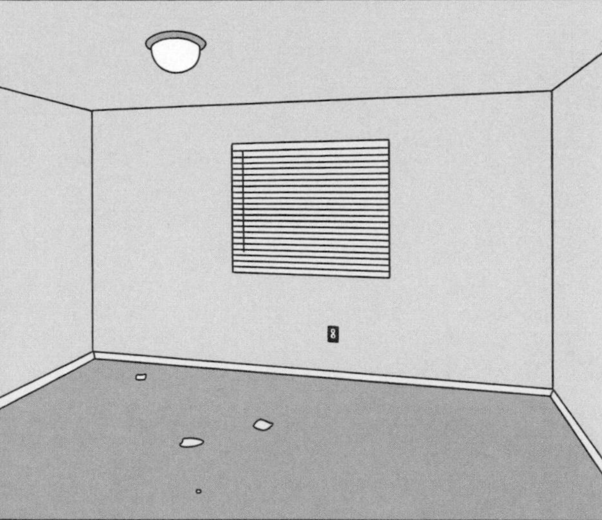

THIS IS JUST THE SPARE BEDROOM.

JACKIE WAS GOING TO MAKE THIS HER WORK ROOM.

IF YOU EVER WANT TO DO ANYTHING IN THERE, BE MY GUEST.

THIS WILL BE YOUR BATHROOM.

I LEFT YOU SOME HYGIENE STUFF IN THE DRAWER. LET ME KNOW IF YOU NEED ANY-THING ELSE.

HERE'S THE LAUNDRY ROOM.

JUST GRAB SOME CLOT-HES IF YOU NEED THEM.

THANKS.

THIS IS MY ROOM.

I'M GONNA SAY THAT MY ROOM IS THE ONLY ONE THAT'S OFF LIMITS.

YOU KNOW I DON'T MIND HAVING YOU HERE AT ALL, I'M JUST WEIRD WITH PERSONAL SPACE.

NO PROBLEM.

I APPRECIATE IT. YOU'RE NOT MISSING ANYTHING.

I'VE GOTTA START GETTING READY.

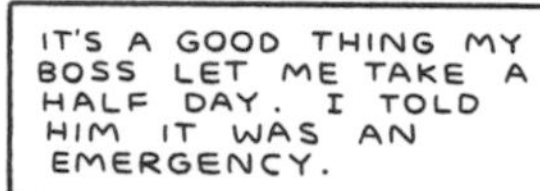
IT'S A GOOD THING MY BOSS LET ME TAKE A HALF DAY. I TOLD HIM IT WAS AN EMERGENCY.

JUST SO YOU KNOW, I WORK MONDAY THROUGH FRIDAY, FOUR TO MIDNIGHT.

THIS WILL BE YOUR ROOM.

THIS WAS CICI'S ROOM.

WE CAN CLEAR SOME OF THIS CRAP OUT.

WHEN THEY LEFT I JUST SHOVED ALL OF HER STUFF IN HERE.

HM.

I HAVEN'T BEEN IN HERE IN A WHILE.

WELL...

I'M SORRY TO RUSH OUT THE DOOR, BUT I REALLY DO HAVE TO GET TO WORK.

OK.

HEY, I DID WANT TO SHOW YOU SOMETHING.

I JUST WANT TO BE UP FRONT ABOUT IT.

I THINK IT MIGHT EVEN PUT YOUR MIND AT EASE.

HOW DO YOU FEEL ABOUT WEAPONS?
WROBEL
U.S. AIR FORC

I ONLY BOUGHT THEM TO PROTECT MY FAMILY.

IF ANYTHING EVER HAPPENS IN THE HOUSE, COME GET ME, AND I'LL TAKE CARE OF IT.

I KEEP THEM IN A LOCKED BAG IN THIS CLOSET, AND I KEEP THE KEY WITH ME AT ALL TIMES.

I JUST WANTED YOU TO KNOW THAT I'M WELL-PROTECTED IF ANYONE TRIES ANY-THING.

OK.

DO YOU NEED ME TO PICK UP ANYTHING ON THE WAY HOME?

NO, THANKS.

ARE YOU GONNA BE ALL RIGHT HERE BY YOURSELF?

YEA.

OK, WELL...

EVERYTHING'S GONNA BE ALL RIGHT.

I'LL SEE YOU LATER.

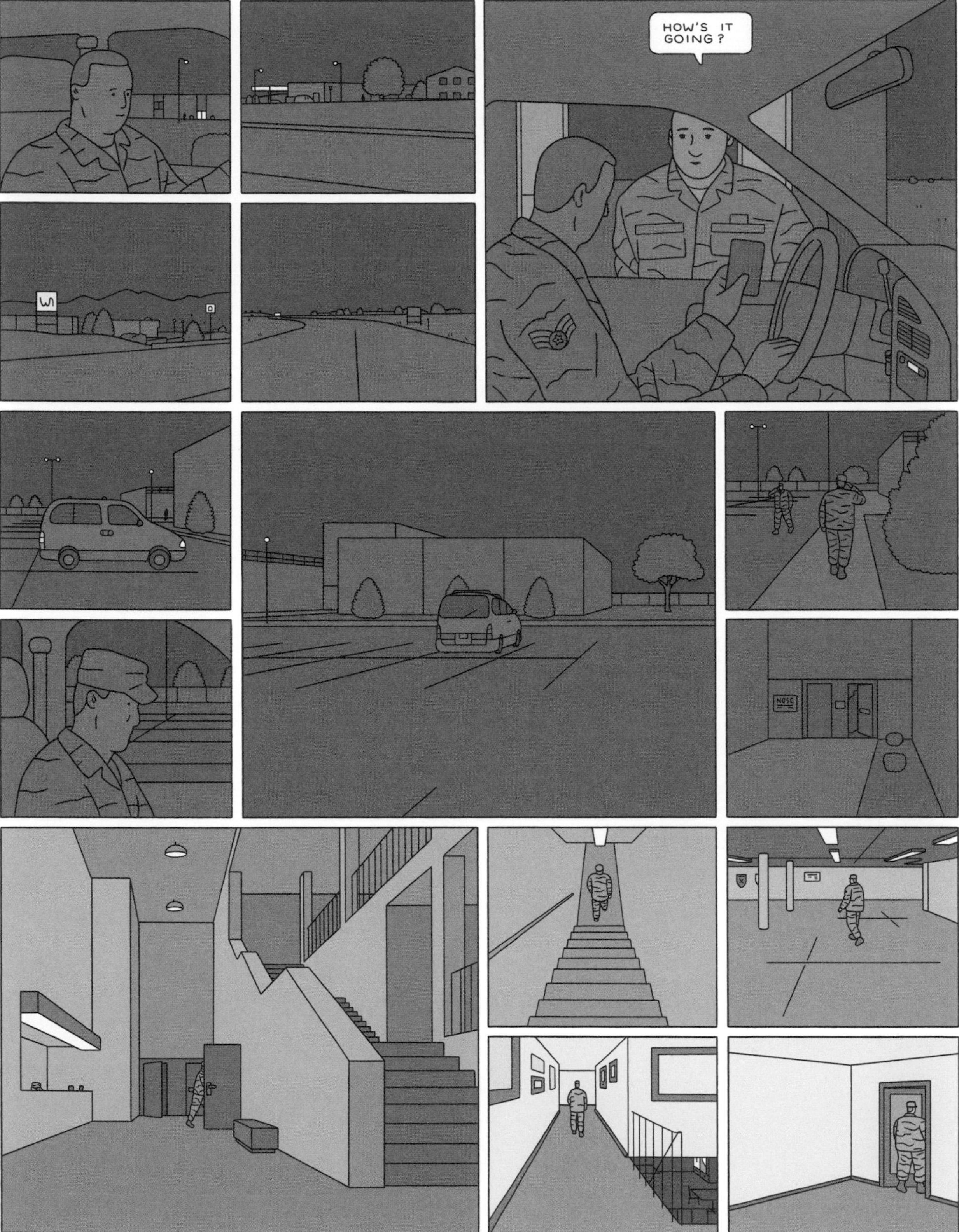
HOW'S IT GOING?

HEY, WROBEL.

HEY.

WHAT'S UP, CALVIN.

HEY, SIMON.

FILL ME IN. I'LL HAVE TO CATCH UP.

WE'RE FINE. IT'S ACTUALLY BEEN PRETTY QUIET TONIGHT.

OH GOOD. SORRY TO LEAVE YOU GUYS HANGING.

NO PROBLEM. I DIDN'T EVEN THINK YOU WERE COMING IN TONIGHT.

SERGEANT SMITH LET ME TAKE A HALF DAY.

I HAD A DOCTOR'S APPOINTMENT THAT SHE HAD TO PUSH BACK TO THE AFTERNOON.

NOTHING SERIOUS. JUST A CHECKUP.

OH. IT'S NO PROBLEM.

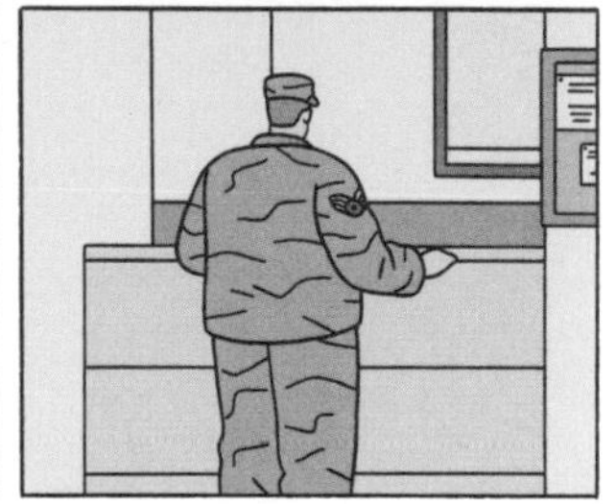

DOD MEDICAL EVALUATION REVIEW BOARD
MENTAL HEALTH SURVEY
PETERSON AIR FORCE BASE COLORADO

DATE: 9/11/17
NAME: SrA Calvin Wrobel

How many hours of sleep did you receive last night?	2-4 ○	4-6 ○	6-8 ●	8-10 ○	10-12 ○
How many alcoholic beverages did you consume last night?	0 ○	1 ○	2 ●	3 ○	4+ ○
Rate your overall mood from 1 to 5, 1 being poor:	1 ○	2 ○	3 ●	4 ○	5 ○
Rate your stress level from 1 to 5, 5 being severe:	1 ○	2 ○	3 ●	4 ○	5 ○
Are you experiencing depression or thoughts of suicide?	Y ○	N ●			

If yes, elaborate: ______

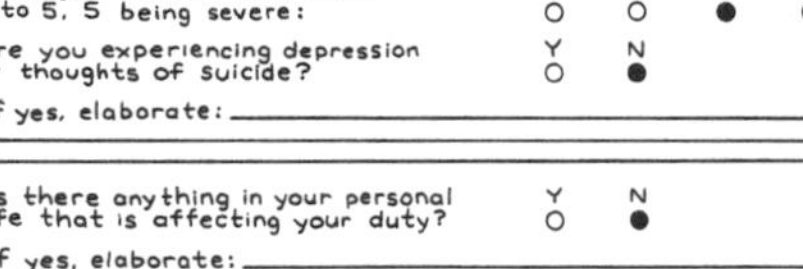

Is there anything in your personal life that is affecting your duty?	Y ○	N ●

If yes, elaborate: ______

Would you like to speak with a clinical psychologist?	Y ○	N ●

Additional Comments: ______

HEY, DO YOU HAVE ANY NEWS FOR ME?

WHAT ARE YOU IN THE MOOD FOR? CURRENT AFFAIRS? SAD? FUNNY? CELEBRITY GOSSIP?

FUNNY, PLEASE. I NEED SOMETHING FUNNY.

FUNNY... FUNNY... HERE WE GO. I FOUND THIS OVER THE WEEKEND. CHECK IT OUT.

THE TITLE IS "PORNO PRODUCT PLACEMENT?"

THE FORMER ADULT FILM STAR KNOWN AS KRIS TAYLOR REPORTED ON HER BLOG THAT SINCE 2014, MAJOR SPONSORS PAID THOUSANDS OF DOLLARS TO COVERTLY PLACE PRODUCTS IN PORNOGRAPHIC FILMS PRODUCED BY THE LOS ANGELES COMPANY SUNKEN TREASURE MEDIA.

TAYLOR HAS IMPLICATED SEVERAL HOUSEHOLD BRANDS, CLAIMING THAT S.T.M. WAS APPROACHED WITH THE OFFERS, ALONG WITH THE EXPLICIT AGREEMENT THAT THEY WOULD REMAIN COMPLETELY SILENT.

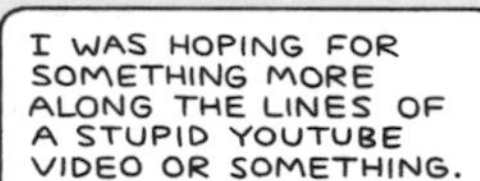
MARLON WILLHELM, DIRECTOR OF SEVERAL OF THE FILMS IN QUESTION, APPEARS TO BE CORROBORATING TAYLOR'S STORY WITH A CRYPTIC REMARK ON TWITTER: "I GUESS THE CAT IS OUT OF THE BAG."

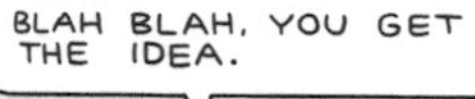
A SPOKESPERSON FOR SARATOGA CHEMICALS, MANUFACTURERS OF THE CLEANING AGENT "GET-OFF" (WHICH CAN BE SEEN CLEARLY IN A SCENE IN THE S.T.M. FILM "HONEY BUNNIES") HAS STATED THAT THEIR COMPANY "IN NO WAY PARTICIPATED IN THIS ARRANGEMENT. OUR PRODUCT WAS USED WITHOUT OUR CONSENT AND WE INTEND TO LITIGATE."

IT IS NOT MADE CLEAR IN HER BLOG ENTRY WHY TAYLOR DECIDED TO REVEAL THE ALLEGED CONSPIRACY, BUT SHE DID EXPRESS CONTEMPT FOR THE PORN INDUSTRY, AND WROTE ABOUT HER INTENTIONS TO TRAVEL, PAINT, AND WRITE AN AUTOBIOGRAPHY.

BLAH BLAH, YOU GET THE IDEA.

PRETTY WEIRD STUFF.

I WAS HOPING FOR SOMETHING MORE ALONG THE LINES OF A STUPID YOUTUBE VIDEO OR SOMETHING.

SEE YOU GUYS LATER.

SEE YA.

YOU KNOW WHAT, I SHOULD REALLY GET BACK TO IT.
DAMMIT.
WHAT'S WRONG?
I'VE GOT THIS REALLY AN-NOYING ITCH ON MY ANKLE, BUT IT'S NOT GO-ING AWAY WHEN I TRY TO SCRATCH IT.
HUH. THAT'S WEIRD.
THE ITCH ON MY ANKLE GOES AWAY WHEN I SCRATCH MY BACK.
THIS IS GOING TO DRIVE ME NUTS!
AH. THAT'S BETTER. DO YOU EVER GET THOSE?
YEA, LIKE A PHANTOM ITCH.
MAYBE I'M JUST GOING CRAZY. IS IT TIME TO GO HOME YET? I'M READY.
HAHA.
HEY, CALVIN.

THEY'RE RUNNING AROUND LIKE CHICKENS WITH THEIR HEADS CUT OFF, I'M TELLING YOU.
FOX

WHAT CAN I DO ABOUT IT?

WHAT'S UP?

I BOUGHT YOU TWO BEERS ON FRIDAY SO YOU OWE ME CIGARETTES THIS WEEK.

IT'S NOT MY JOB TO DO THEIR JOB. NO SHIT.

CHIN-SUN'S BROTHER IS STAYING WITH US.

I DROVE US TO THE TOP OF PIKES PEAK ON SATURDAY. HAVE YOU EVER DONE THAT? JESUS CHRIST.

FIRST OF ALL, HER BROTHER NO-YE SPEAKS, LIKE, NO ENGLISH.

ALSO, I LEARNED THAT I'M TERRIFIED OF HEIGHTS.

THE ROAD WINDS UP THE CLIFFS WITH NO GUARD-RAILS. I WAS TRYING TO REMAIN CALM BECAUSE I WANTED TO MAKE A GOOD IMPRESSION ON HIM.

THEY LOVED IT, BUT I WAS LOSING MY MIND. THEY WERE SPOTTING RAMS AND HAWKS WHILE I WAS TRY-ING NOT TO THROW UP.

EVEN IF I WANTED TO GO BACK DOWN, IT'S THIS NARROW ROAD AND THERE'S NO PLACE TO TURN AROUND. I WAS TRAPPED!

ON THE RIDE HOME I'M PRETTY SURE HE WAS MAKING FUN OF ME IN KOREAN.

DON'T DESPAIR
This machine *is* temperamental but it will give you change for your dollar bill if you persevere.

CONNOR?

AH.

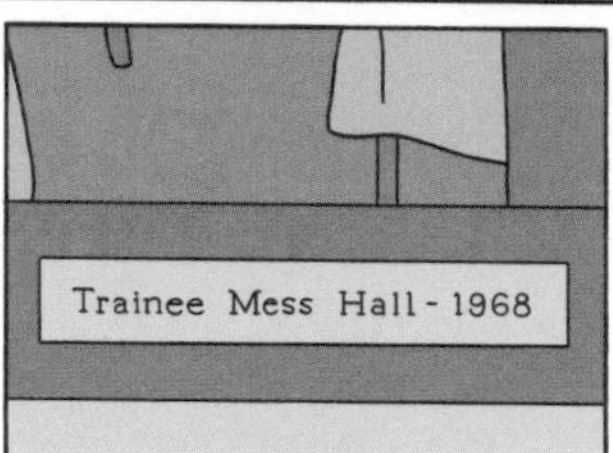

SORRY, CAL. I HAD TO TAKE THAT PHONE CALL. COME ON BACK!

SERGEANT HEFFER TOOK OFF FOR THE NIGHT SO WE CAN SPREAD OUT BACK HERE.

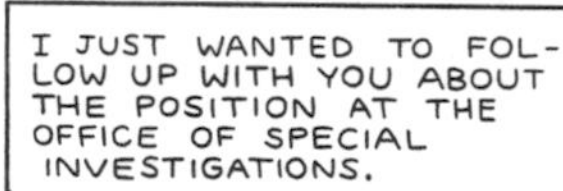

I JUST WANTED TO FOL-LOW UP WITH YOU ABOUT THE POSITION AT THE OFFICE OF SPECIAL INVESTIGATIONS.

OH.
COLONEL TUCKER ASKED ABOUT YOU AGAIN. HE STILL THINKS YOU WOULD BE A PRIME CANDIDATE, AND HE WANTED ME TO SEE WHERE YOU WERE AT.

I'M CERTAINLY HONORED. REALLY.

IT'S A BIG DECISION. I KNOW.

I JUST HAVE A LOT OF PERSONAL STUFF I NEED TO TAKE CARE OF AFTER I'M DISCHARGED.

WELL, AS I'M SURE HE TOLD YOU, IT'S A THREE YEAR MINIMUM IN O.S.I.

I KNOW. HE WENT OVER THE BARE BONES OF THE CONTRACT. HONESTLY, IT WAS A LITTLE SCARY.

HOW SO?

I'M SORRY TO HEAR THAT. WE'VE ALL MADE OUR SACRIFICES THOUGH.

MY DAUGHTER IS ALREADY FOUR. THE PROSPECT OF MOVING TO VIRGINIA, AND BEING DISPATCHED ANY-WHERE IN THE WORLD FOR MONTHS AT A TIME, AND BEING FORBIDDEN TO CON-TACT MY FAMILY. I DON'T KNOW IF I CAN DO IT.

MY WIFE AND DAUGHTER ARE LIVING WITH HER PARENTS IN FLORIDA. I'M TRYING TO RECONCILE WITH HER AND MOVE THERE WHEN I GET OUT NEXT SPRING, IF SHE WANTS ME.

ALL I ASK IS THAT YOU CONSIDER IT. IT'S A CHANCE TO MOVE UP TO THE NEXT LEVEL. IF YOU'RE THINKING "CAREER," THIS COULD REALLY OPEN DOORS FOR YOU.

AND IN THREE YEARS, YOU'RE OUT. YOU CAN GO WHEREVER YOU WANT.

JUST REMEMBER THAT CRISIS LEADS TO OPPORTUNITY.

I DON'T KNOW. I REALLY HAVE TO THINK ABOUT IT.

THAT'S PERFECTLY UNDER-STANDABLE. I WON'T PUSH TOO HARD.

SO WHAT HAPPENED TODAY? YOU SAID YOU HAVE AN OLD FRIEND STAYING WITH YOU WHO'S GOING THROUGH SOME KIND OF CRISIS OF HIS OWN?
SMITH
U.S.

YEA, MY OLD FRIEND FROM ILLINOIS. IT'S A WEIRD THING. HIS GIRLFRIEND IS MISSING.

MISSING? WHAT HAPPENED?

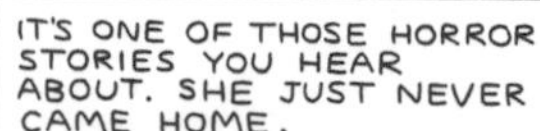
IT'S ONE OF THOSE HORROR STORIES YOU HEAR ABOUT. SHE JUST NEVER CAME HOME.

OH NO.

THEY EVEN GOT HER ON A SECURITY CAMERA A BLOCK AWAY FROM THEIR APARTMENT WALKING HOME FROM WORK AT HER USUAL TIME, AND AFTER THAT, NOTHING.

THAT IS STRANGE. WHEN WAS THIS?
A MONTH AGO.

YEA.
HE HAD SOME KIND OF NERVOUS BREAKDOWN, SO HIS PARENTS ASKED IF HE COULD COME STAY WITH ME. I SAID "SURE THING" EVEN THOUGH WE LOST TOUCH AFTER HIGH SCHOOL.

UH-OH.
WELL I COMMEND YOU FOR HELPING OUT A FRIEND.
CAN YOU KEEP THIS BETWEEN US? I TOLD THE GUYS I HAD A DOCTOR'S APPOINTMENT.

NO PROBLEM, BUT I REALLY DON'T FIND IT NECESSARY TO DECEIVE YOUR FELLOW AIRMEN.

I KNOW, I'M SORRY. I JUST DIDN'T WANT TO HAVE A LITTLE PRESS CONFERENCE IN THE OFFICE.

THESE GUYS WOULD LITERALLY TAKE A BULLET FOR YOU. I'M SURE THEY'D BE JUST AS CONCERNED AS I AM ABOUT YOU AND YOUR FRIEND'S WELL-BEING. MAYBE THEY CAN HELP.

AND OBVIOUSLY, IF YOU NEED ANYTHING AT ALL FROM ME, DON'T HESITATE. MY DOOR IS ALWAYS OPEN. JUST REMEMBER THAT YOU HAVE YOUR RESPONSIBILITIES HERE.

THANKS, ED. I APPRECIATE THAT.

WHAT WAS HER NAME, BY THE WAY? I'D LIKE TO FOLLOW THE STORY.
SABRINA GALLO.

THERE HAVEN'T BEEN ANY NEW DEVELOPMENTS. ALL THE ARTICLES ARE FROM LAST MONTH.

THE FAMILY HAS A LITTLE FACEBOOK PAGE, BUT THAT'S ABOUT IT.

I'LL BE PRAYING FOR HER. KEEP ME ABREAST, ALL RIGHT?

YOU GOT IT.

WOULD YOU SHUT THAT DOOR FOR ME ON YOUR WAY OUT?

HAVE A GOOD NIGHT.

WHERE ARE YOU GOING, DAHLMAN?

WE'RE ALL GOING OVER TO KELLY'S TO PLAY. DID YOU CHANGE YOUR MIND?

NO, I SHOULD REALLY GET HOME.

I'VE GOTTA SEE THE SERGEANT ABOUT SOME-THING. MEET YOU THERE.

COME ON, CAL. YOU'RE NOT UP FOR A LITTLE 'BLACK OPS?'

NAH. I'M MORE OF A 'WORLD OF WARFARE' MAN MYSELF.

HEY.

I PICKED UP SOME GOODIES.

WHAT A DAY.

HEY, RANDY.

YOU SHOULD EAT SOME-THING. I'LL BRING YOU A PLATE.

THIS IS THE ONLY DECENT PIZZA AROUND HERE. THEY CALL IT "CHICAGO-STYLE." HA-HA.

I BOUGHT SOMETHING CALLED 'SERFS UP! REBEL PALE ALE.' I HAVEN'T TRIED THIS ONE YET.

I'M A SUCKER FOR MICRO-BREWS. I LIKE THAT BRAND. THEY HAVE COOL PACKAGING.

HERE YOU GO.

THANKS.

NAPKINS.

OH BOY.

REMEMBER THAT KID THAT USED TO SAY GRACE BEFORE LUNCH IN JUNIOR HIGH?

RAY RAMONDI.
HEH - WHATEVER HAPPENED TO HIM?

MM. PRETTY GOOD.

YEA. IT'S NOT BAD.

REMEMBER HISTORY CLASS WITH MISS WAX?

THAT WAS THE FIRST TIME WE BECAME, I GUESS YOU COULD SAY, REAL FRIENDS.

YOU USED TO SIT SO QUIETLY IN THE BACK ROW.

UNTIL THAT DAY WE WERE WATCHING A VIDEO ABOUT THE AMERICAN REVOLUTION. THERE WAS A COMMERCIAL IN IT FOR SODA POP AND YOU FREAKED OUT.
I JUST REMEMBER YOU SCREECHING "I WILL NOT BE ADVERTISED TO IN A PLACE OF LEARNING!"

HAHA.

NOBODY UNDERSTOOD WHY YOU WERE GETTING SO MAD. I JUST THOUGHT IT WAS HILARIOUS.

YEA, I REMEMBER THAT.

ANYWAY, I WAS JUST THINKING ABOUT THAT ON THE DRIVE TO WORK. IT MADE ME LAUGH.

WHAT'S THAT?

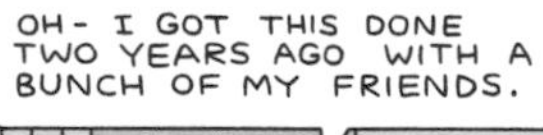
OH - I GOT THIS DONE TWO YEARS AGO WITH A BUNCH OF MY FRIENDS.

COOL.

I NEVER THOUGHT I WOULD BE A TATTOO PERSON.

ON OUR LAST FAMILY VACATION IN CANCUN, I ENDED UP MEETING THIS RETIRED LIEUTENANT IN THE HOTEL BAR.

WHEN HE SPOTTED MY TATTOO HE BOUGHT ME A SHOT, AND WE ENDED UP SPENDING THE WHOLE TRIP WITH HIM AND HIS WIFE, JUST HAVING THE BEST TIME.
WE STILL KEEP IN TOUCH.

THAT'S NICE. YOUR OWN FRATERNAL BROTHERHOOD.

I SUPPOSE.

MM. I LOVE THIS PIZZA. WANT SOME MORE?

I'M ALL RIGHT.

I'M GONNA CHANGE REAL QUICK.

OK- PROMISE YOU WON'T MAKE FUN OF ME.

WHAT IS THAT?

IT'S ONE OF THOSE SLEEVED BLANKETS YOU SEE ON TELEVISION.

WITNESS MY SAD LITTLE NIGHTLY RITUAL.

IT LOOKS GOOD.

HAHA, SURE. I GOT IT AS A GAG GIFT AT THE WORK CHRISTMAS PARTY, BUT GODDAMMIT, I WEAR THIS STUPID THING EVERY NIGHT.

SMOKE?

SURE.

I'M NOT SUPPOSED TO SMOKE IN THE CONDO, BUT WHATEVER. RULES ARE MEANT TO BE BROKEN.

WHEN ARE YOU MOVING?

NO.

THAT'S ALL RIGHT. I DON'T EITHER.

APRIL. SO YOU COULD EVEN STAY UNTIL THEN IF YOU REALLY WANT. DO YOU HAVE A PLAN?

I THOUGHT YOU WERE GOING TO FLORIDA?

YEA. I NEED TO BE CLOSE TO CICI. I'M NOT GONNA BE ONE OF THOSE DADS WHO SENDS A CHECK EVERY MONTH. NO FUCKING WAY.

TWO OF MY BUDDIES ARE MOVING THERE WHEN THEY GET OUT NEXT YEAR AND WE'RE TALKING ABOUT STARTING A SECURITY COMPANY.

YEA, ME TOO.

HONESTLY THOUGH, I DON'T KNOW IF JACKIE EVEN WANTS ME AROUND.

I THOUGHT EVERYTHING WAS FINE.

REMEMBER THAT ONE NIGHT WE WERE TALKING ON THE PHONE?

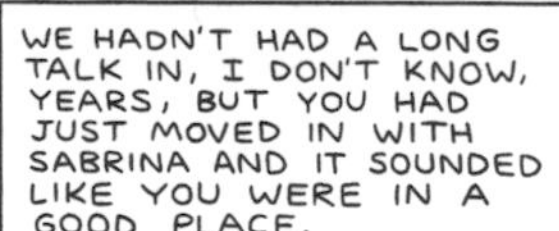
WE HADN'T HAD A LONG TALK IN, I DON'T KNOW, YEARS, BUT YOU HAD JUST MOVED IN WITH SABRINA AND IT SOUNDED LIKE YOU WERE IN A GOOD PLACE.

I WAS THE MARRIED GUY GIVING YOU ADVICE ABOUT HOW TO LIVE WITH YOUR GIRLFRIEND. I THOUGHT WE HAD A NICE TALK, AND I HUNG UP FEELING SELF-ASSURED AND HAPPY FOR YOU.

THE NEXT DAY SHE LEFT ME. SHE SAID I WAS OBLIVIOUS AND DETACHED. I GUESS I CAN'T ARGUE WITH THAT.

HM.

I JUST WANT HER TO COME BACK.
THIS CAN'T BE HAPPENING.
DEAR GOD.
WHAT HAPPENED?
WHERE IS SHE?!

I'M SO SORRY.
AH!
I HAVEN'T KEPT DOWN A MEAL ALL MONTH.

AH! IS THERE A BATH- ROOM DOWN HERE?

AROUND THE CORNER.

I SWEAR TO GOD, IF THEY FIND WHOEVER IS RESPONSIBLE, I AM GOING TO KILL HIM.

I'M SERIOUS. I AM GOING TO KILL HIM.

AND IF HE'S DEAD... AND SHE'S DEAD, I'M JUST GOING TO KILL MYSELF. THAT'S THE TRUTH.

YEA, I MEAN, I TOTALLY UNDERSTAND. I'M SURE I WOULD FEEL THE SAME WAY.

YEA.

WANNA WATCH SOMETHING?

[Somber music]

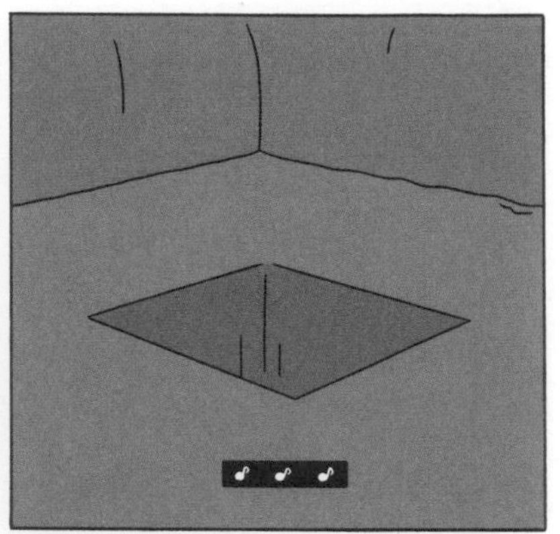

>> Welcome back to this special edition of nightly news.
>> It is of course the sixteenth anniversary of the 9-1-1 attacks.

>> We are here at ground zero, now the location of the 9-1-1 museum and 9-1-1 memorial, which opened to the public six years ago today on the tenth anniversary of the attacks.

>> A tranquil oasis of tribute and remembrance, mourners gather at the two large reflecting pools, great chasms built into the footprint of where the World Trade Center used to stand.

>> Conflicted emotions at the memorial, where families leave flowers, flags, and tributes to loved ones lost.

[Street noise]

>> With the big 2-0 just a few years away, organizers have teased the possibility of a live concert at the memorial for the twenty-year anniversary.

>> I cannot believe how long it's been.
>> Believe it or not, I was in fourth grade on 9-1-1.

>> Now I work in the Freedom Tower.

[Somber music]

>> Inside the memorial museum, we travel seven stories below street level, right down to the bedrock on which the Twin Towers once stood.

8:46
>> A tour of the museum is a virtual history of vivid sights and sounds designed to transport visitors back to that day.

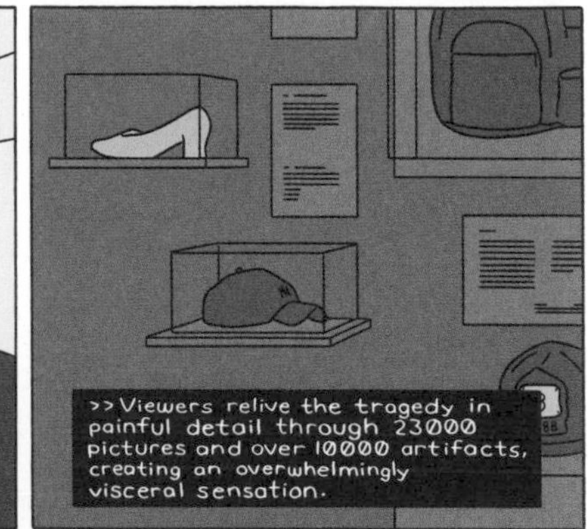
>> Viewers relive the tragedy in painful detail through 23000 pictures and over 10000 artifacts, creating an overwhelmingly visceral sensation.

NO DAY SHALL ERASE YOU

SE YOU FROM THE MEMORY OF TIME
Virgil
>> Behind this wall is a repository housing some 8000 unidentified human remains.

>> My sister died on Flight 1-7-5. The grief stays with me every day.

>> Our goal is to pay tribute to the ones that were lost that day. The heroes, the first responders, the innocent victims.

>> We want guests to leave with an increased sense of the value of a human life, that each one is important and won't be forgotten.

>> It was an event that changed life as we know it forever. It's our duty to preserve that moment for people a hundred years from now.

>> This is a sacred place. A part of history.

>> After touring the museum, I definitely have a greater appreciation for the sacrifices that were made here.

>> Like every American, I have a lot of personal memories wrapped up in 9-1-1. It is important to look back and reflect on how far we've come.

TAKE A NICE STROLL DOWN MEMORY LANE AT THE NINE-ELEVEN MUSEUM.

REMEMBER DREW PETERSON? THAT COP THAT KILLED HIS WIVES? IT WAS A BIG NEWS STORY IN 2007.

I WAS DATING EMMA THAT SUMMER. WE USED TO SIT IN HER MOM'S BASEMENT AND WATCH MOVIES ALL NIGHT.

WE WERE WATCHING A TV SPECIAL ABOUT DREW PETERSON ONE NIGHT WHEN WE LEANED IN AND KISSED EACH OTHER FOR THE FIRST TIME.

NOW WHENEVER I SEE OR HEAR ANYTHING ABOUT DREW PETERSON, I FEEL LIKE I'M EIGHTEEN IN EMMA'S BASEMENT AGAIN.

IS IT WEIRD TO FEEL NOSTALGIC FOR STUFF LIKE THAT?

HEH... NEVERMIND.

LET'S GET YOU TO BED, BUDDY.
MM.

COME ON- I'LL HELP YOU.

HUP!

ATTA BOY. TAKE IT SLOW.

HERE WE GO.
LEMME MOVE THIS SHIT OFF THE BED.
ARE YOU STILL WITH ME?
MMM..
LET'S WASH THESE CLOTHES SINCE THEY'RE ALL YOU HAVE.
TEDDY, DO YOU WANT ANYTHING? PAJAMAS? A BLANKET?
HMM..
I'M ON THE OTHER SIDE OF THAT WALL IF YOU NEED ANYTHING.

HEY DAHLMAN. U STILL UP?
BESTBUDDY89
LOOK WHO IT IS.
SINISTERCD89
I WAS JUST ABOUT TO SIGN OFF, BUT WHO DO I SEE SIGNING ON...
HAHA, YEA. WHAT CAN I SAY...
JUST WOKE UP AND I CAN'T FALL BACK ASLEEP. KILLING PEOPLE ALWAYS PUTS ME TO SLEEP ;)
COULDA USED YOUR HELP TONIGHT...

AH, I'M SORRY. DID YOU GUYS DO ALRIGHT?
WE GOT FUCKING SLAUGHTERED. WE WERE TOTALLY OUTNUMBERED.
SHIT. I'LL BE ON TOMORROW AND WE'LL GET SOME PAYBACK.
ARE YOU STAYING ON?
MAYBE.
WHOA IT'S 3 AM. I'M GONNA TRY TO GO BACK TO SLEEP.
ALRIGHT.
I'LL SEE YOU TOMORROW.
YUP.
Jackie
Cancun 2015

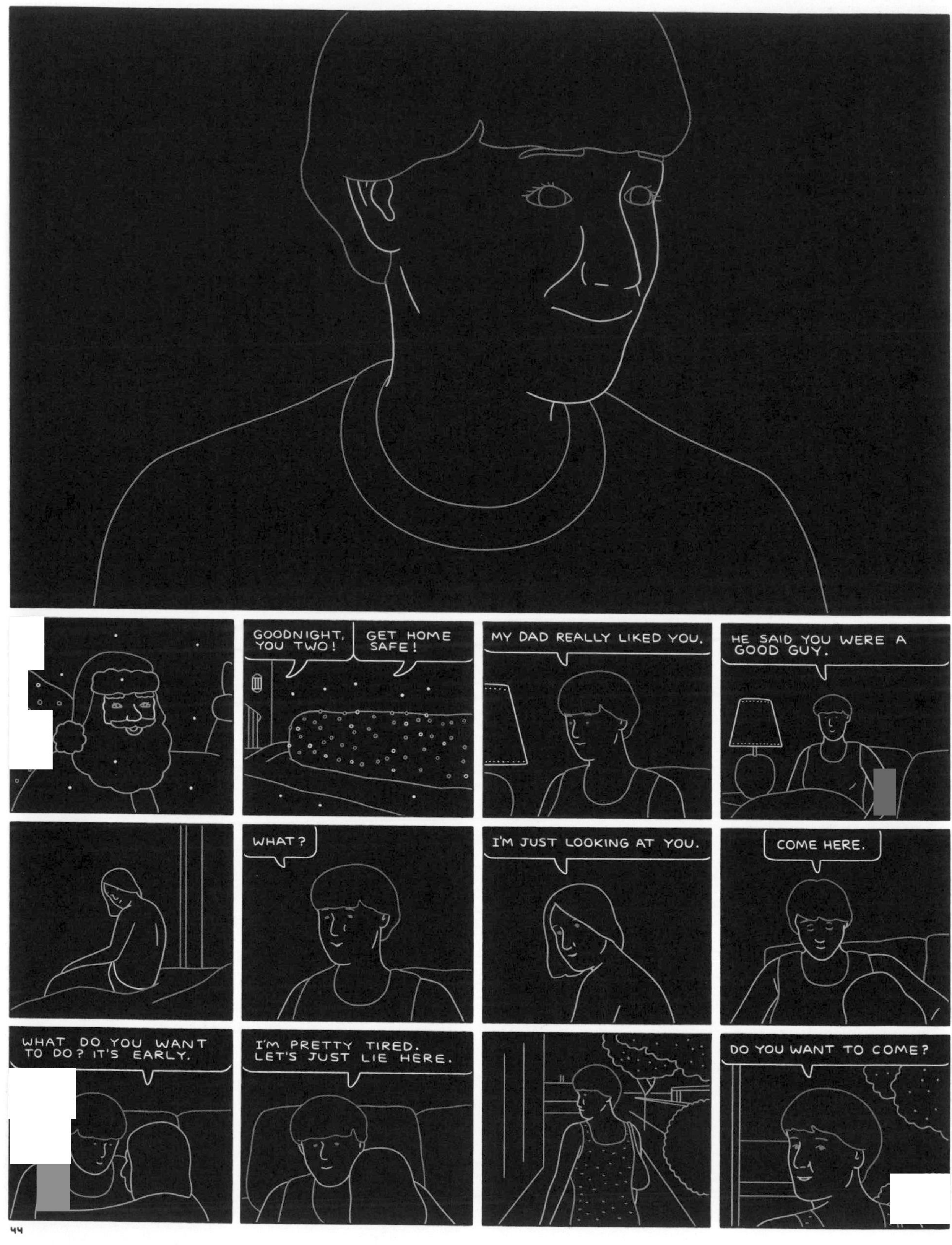
GOODNIGHT, YOU TWO!
GET HOME SAFE!
MY DAD REALLY LIKED YOU.
HE SAID YOU WERE A GOOD GUY.
WHAT?
I'M JUST LOOKING AT YOU.
COME HERE.
WHAT DO YOU WANT TO DO? IT'S EARLY.
I'M PRETTY TIRED. LET'S JUST LIE HERE.
DO YOU WANT TO COME?

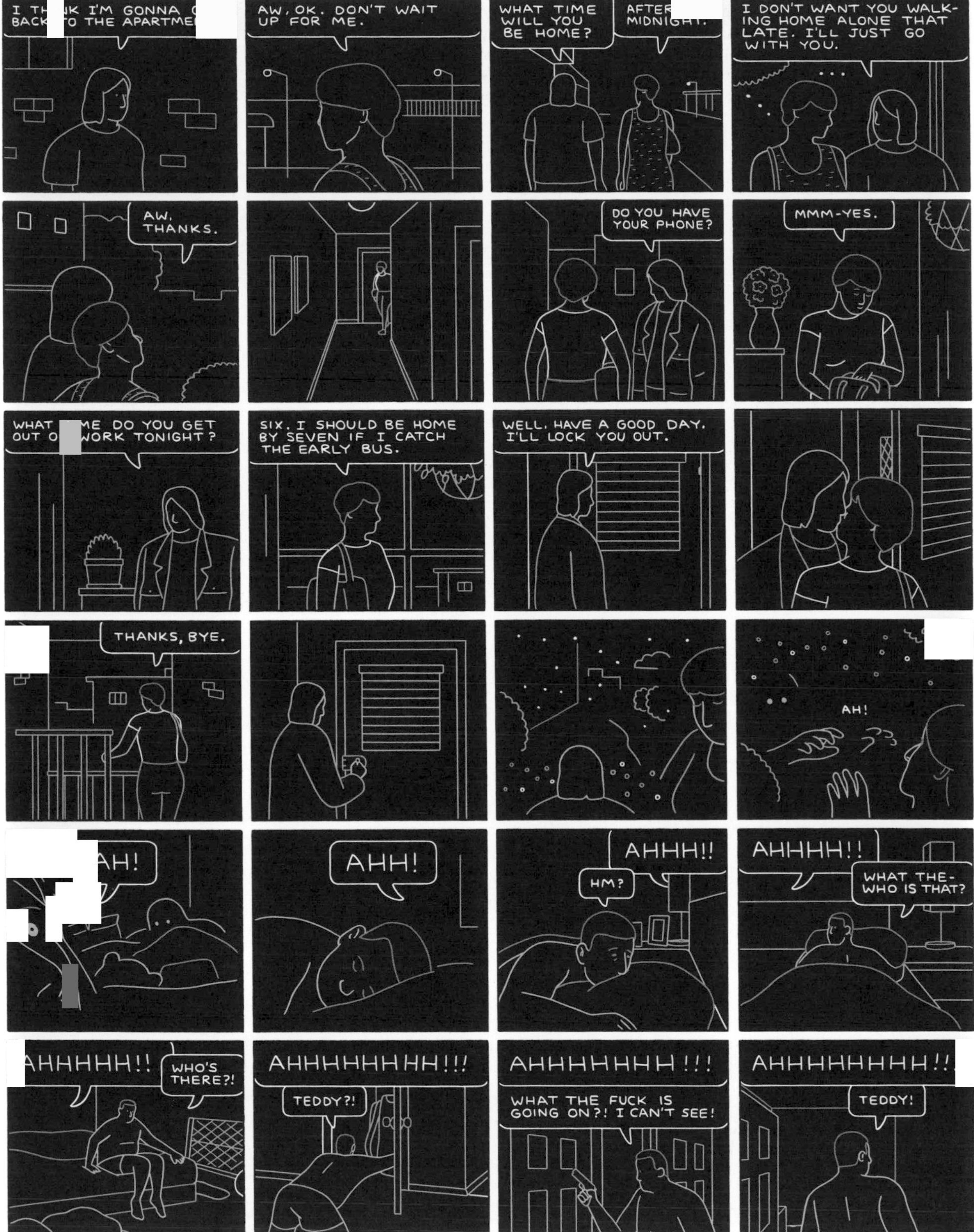
I TH K I'M GONNA
BACK O THE APARTME
AW, OK. DON'T WAIT UP FOR ME.
WHAT TIME WILL YOU BE HOME?
AFTER MIDNIG
I DON'T WANT YOU WALK-ING HOME ALONE THAT LATE. I'LL JUST GO WITH YOU.
...
AW. THANKS.
DO YOU HAVE YOUR PHONE?
MMM-YES.
WHAT ME DO YOU GET OUT O WORK TONIGHT?
SIX. I SHOULD BE HOME BY SEVEN IF I CATCH THE EARLY BUS.
WELL, HAVE A GOOD DAY. I'LL LOCK YOU OUT.
THANKS, BYE.
AH!
AH!
AHH!
AHHH!!
HM?
AHHHH!!
WHAT THE- WHO IS THAT?
AHHHHH!!
WHO'S THERE?!
AHHHHHHHH!!!
TEDDY?!
AHHHHHHHH!!!
WHAT THE FUCK IS GOING ON?! I CAN'T SEE!
AHHHHHHHHH!!
TEDDY!

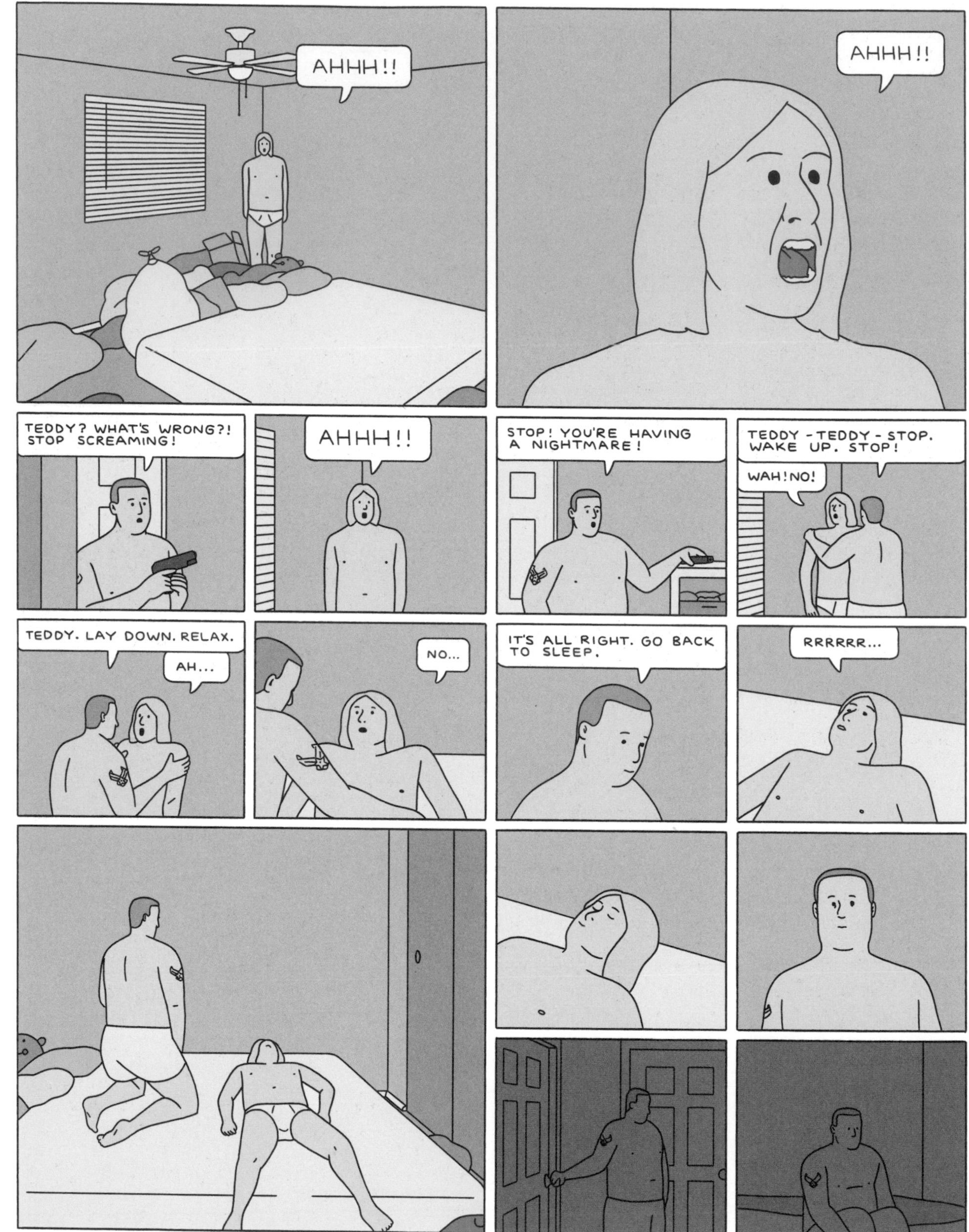
AHHH!!
AHHH!!
TEDDY? WHAT'S WRONG?! STOP SCREAMING!
AHHH!!
STOP! YOU'RE HAVING A NIGHTMARE!
TEDDY - TEDDY - STOP. WAKE UP. STOP!
WAH! NO!
TEDDY. LAY DOWN. RELAX.
AH...
NO...
IT'S ALL RIGHT. GO BACK TO SLEEP.
RRRRRR...

JESUS.
CALVIN?
HEY, JACKIE. DID I WAKE YOU?
NO, NO. WHAT'S WRONG?
NOTHING. I JUST WANTED TO TALK TO CICI. IS SHE THERE?
CICI! COME DOWN HERE! DADDY!
HAVE YOU BEEN UP ALL NIGHT?
NO. I JUST GOT UP EARLY TO DO SOME CHORES BEFORE WORK.
HOW HAVE YOU BEEN?
GREAT. MY MOM AND I HAVE A LOT TO DO WITH CICI TODAY.
THAT'S GREAT. KEEPING BUSY.
YEA, SO I'VE GOTTA START GETTING READY. SHE'S COMING RIGHT NOW.
OK. WELL-
HI, DADDY!

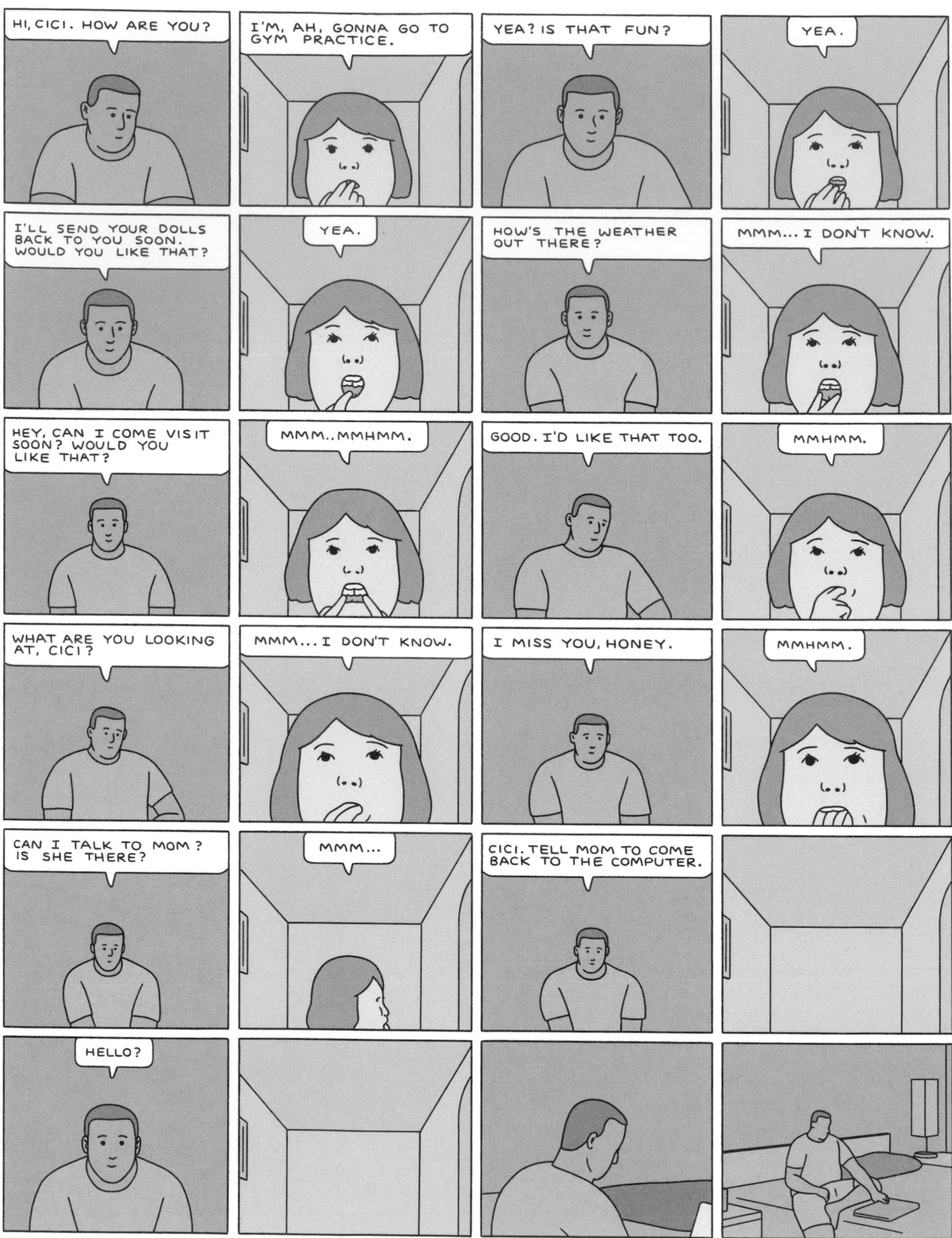
HI, CICI. HOW ARE YOU?
I'M, AH, GONNA GO TO GYM PRACTICE.
YEA? IS THAT FUN?
YEA.
I'LL SEND YOUR DOLLS BACK TO YOU SOON. WOULD YOU LIKE THAT?
YEA.
HOW'S THE WEATHER OUT THERE?
MMM... I DON'T KNOW.
HEY, CAN I COME VISIT SOON? WOULD YOU LIKE THAT?
MMM..MMHMM.
GOOD. I'D LIKE THAT TOO.
MMHMM.
WHAT ARE YOU LOOKING AT, CICI?
MMM... I DON'T KNOW.
I MISS YOU, HONEY.
MMHMM.
CAN I TALK TO MOM? IS SHE THERE?
MMM...
CICI. TELL MOM TO COME BACK TO THE COMPUTER.
HELLO?

11:34
6 Missed Calls
Unknown #
...
TED?
HELLO?

Incoming
312-60
HELLO?
IS THIS CALVIN WROBEL?
YES?
CAN I SPEAK TO TEDDY?
I, UH... I'M NOT SURE WHERE HE IS AT THE MOMENT. WHO IS THIS?
OH GOD. OH MY GOD...
CALM DOWN. WHO IS THIS?
MY... UM... OH GOD!
WHO IS THIS?!
-SNF- MY NAME IS SANDRA. I'M SABRINA'S SISTER.
OH GOD. I'M SO SORRY. WHAT'S GOING ON?
IT'S, UM...
OH NO.
WE GOT A LETTER AT MY PARENTS' HOUSE.
IT HAD SABRINA'S BUS PASS IN IT.

NEIGH-BORHOOD WATCH
HEY! WHAT'S YOUR NAME?
WHAT IS YOUR NAME?
TEDDY.
IF YOU SEE A KID NAMED LOGAN, TELL HIM I'M OUT FOR HIS BLOOD.
LOGAN

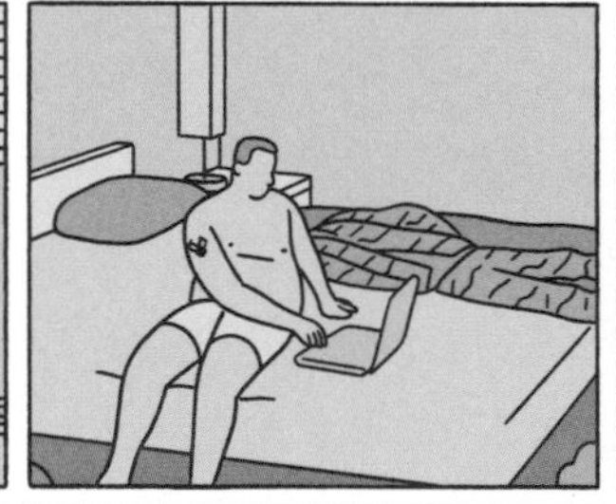

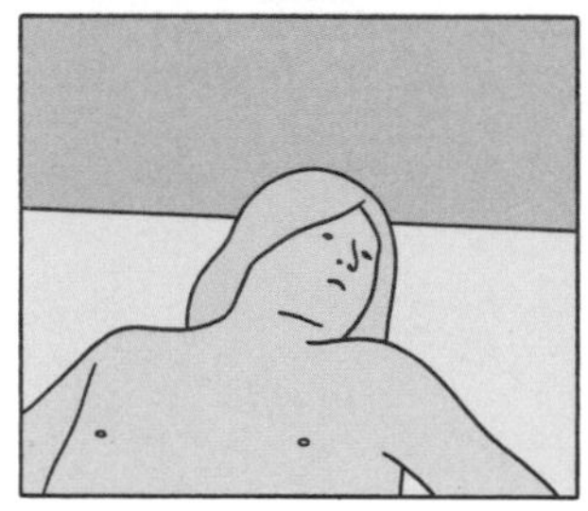

DOD MEDICAL EVALUATION REVIEW BOARD
MENTAL HEALTH SURVEY
PETERSON AIR FORCE BASE COLORADO

DATE: 9/12/17
NAME: SrA Calvin Wrobel

How many hours of sleep did you receive last night?	2-4 ○	4-6 ●	6-8 ○	8-10 ○	10-12 ○
How many alcoholic beverages did you consume last night?	0 ○	1 ○	2 ○	3 ●	4+ ○
Rate your overall mood from 1 to 5, 1 being poor:	1 ○	2 ●	3 ○	4 ○	5 ○
Rate your stress level from 1 to 5, 5 being severe:	1 ○	2 ○	3 ○	4 ●	5 ○
Are you experiencing depression or thoughts of suicide?	Y ○	N ●			

If yes, elaborate: ____________________

Is there anything in your personal life that is affecting your duty?	Y ○	N ●

If yes, elaborate: ____________________

Would you like to speak with a clinical psychologist?	Y ○	N ●

Additional Comments: ____________________

ABCDEFGHIJKLMNOPQRSTUVWXYZ

HEY, TEDDY.

YOU FOUND CICI'S FAV-
ORITE BOOK.
USAF

HUNGRY?

NO.

LISTEN...

I DON'T EVEN KNOW WHAT TO SAY ABOUT THAT LETTER.

IT'S AWFUL. I CAN'T STOP THINKING ABOUT IT.

JESUS.

MAYBE IT'S SOME KIND OF GOOD SIGN. BEFORE THAT, WE ALL ASSUMED THE WORST ALREADY HAPPENED.

I DON'T KNOW.

DO YOU THINK MAYBE THERE'S SOMETHING WE'RE MISSING?

WHAT DO YOU MEAN?

I DON'T KNOW. WE AS-SUME WE ARE DEALING WITH A STRAIGHT-UP ABDUCTION, OR A RAN-SOM. MAYBE THERE'S A MORE COMPLICATED EXPLANATION.

WHAT DOES THAT MEAN?

I'M JUST SAYING WE DON'T KNOW WHAT THE HELL HAPPENED, SO THE BUS PASS DOESN'T REALLY MEAN ANY-THING YET.

I HOPE SO.

JESUS. YOUR LIPS ARE ALL CRACKED. HAVE YOU HAD ANYTHING TO DRINK ALL DAY?

SURE! LOOK AT PATTY HEARST. ANYTHING IS POSSIBLE.

I GUESS SO.

HAVE SOME SODA.

DO YOU STILL LIKE CHEESEBURGERS WITH JUST KETCHUP?

YEA, THANKS.

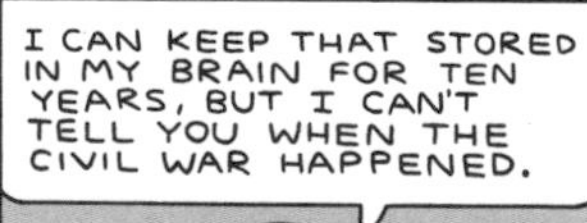
I CAN KEEP THAT STORED IN MY BRAIN FOR TEN YEARS, BUT I CAN'T TELL YOU WHEN THE CIVIL WAR HAPPENED.

WHAT'S WRONG WITH IT?
NOTHING.
I'M HAVING TROUBLE MOVING.
HERE. YOU GOTTA EAT SOMETHING, MAN.
THERE WE GO.
I'M SORRY.
YOU HAVE NOTHING TO BE SORRY ABOUT. I'M HERE TO HELP YOU.
CALVIN?

JESUS CHRIST!
YOU SCARED THE SHIT OUT OF ME.
WHAT ARE YOU DOING?
I THOUGHT I HEARD A RAT IN THE ATTIC.
A RAT?
YEA. I DIDN'T SEE ANY-THING.
WHAT ARE YOU DOING AWAKE?

I JUST WANTED TO SAY THANK YOU FOR LETTING ME STAY WITH YOU.

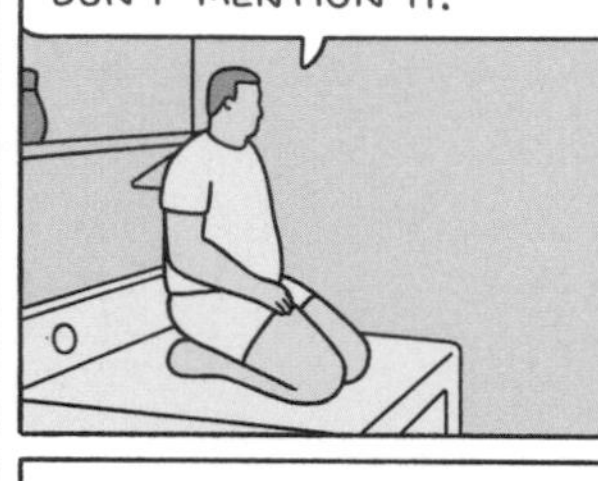
OH. YEA, OF COURSE. DON'T MENTION IT.

I REALLY APPRECIATE IT.

IT'S NO TROUBLE AT ALL, TEDDY. I MEAN THAT.
WELL, GOODNIGHT.

YEA.

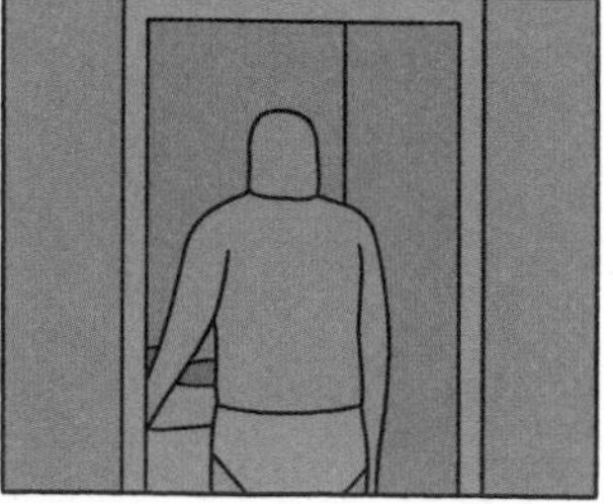

KNOCK
KNOCK
ANNA?
YEA.
HOLD ON.
HOW ARE YOU DOING?
-SNF-
IT'S
OK..

WHAT DO YOU NEED? WATER? AN ICE PACK?

HERE.

YOUR HANDS ARE SHAKING LIKE CRAZY.

THE DOCTOR GAVE ME SOMETHING FOR THAT.

IS IT HELPING?

NO.

LET'S SIT DOWN. CAN YOU STAY FOR A WHILE?

YEA. I CAN STAY AS LONG AS YOU NEED ME.

HAVE PEOPLE BEEN HERE WITH YOU?

MY AUNT'S COMING OVER TOMORROW MORNING, BUT SHE HAS TO LEAVE AT TWO. THEN SUZANNE IS GONNA TRY TO STOP BY AFTER WORK.

DO YOU HAVE A BACKUP? I MIGHT BE ABLE TO COME BACK.

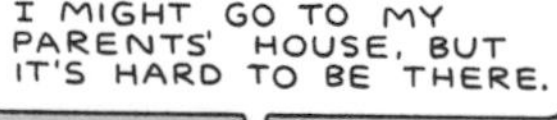
I MIGHT GO TO MY PARENTS' HOUSE, BUT IT'S HARD TO BE THERE.

YEA.

THE LAST TIME I SAW HER SHE WAS WATCHING THEIR CATS. THAT WAS TWO DAYS BEFORE SHE DISAPPEARED.

SORRY, I CAN'T SIT HERE. I DON'T KNOW WHAT TO DO.

I'M SERIOUS. I DON'T KNOW WHAT TO DO!
GOD, I DON'T KNOW WHAT TO DO.

HEY, COME HERE.

SIT ON THE GROUND LIKE THIS.

LET'S TRY SOMETHING.

I'M NOT SURE WHAT I'M DO-ING. LET'S SEE.

LEAN YOUR BODY BACK AND REST AGAINST ME.

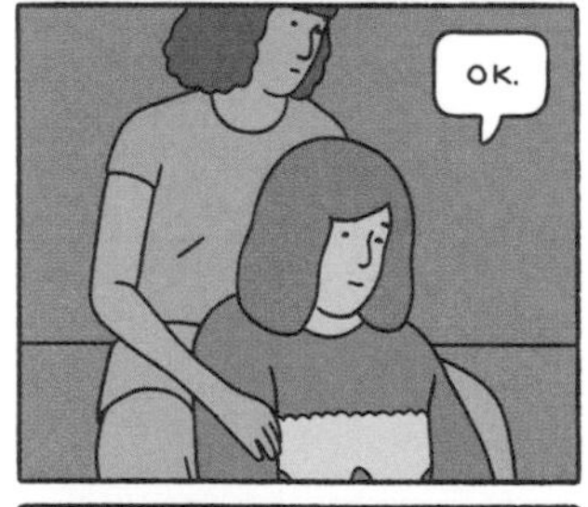
OK.
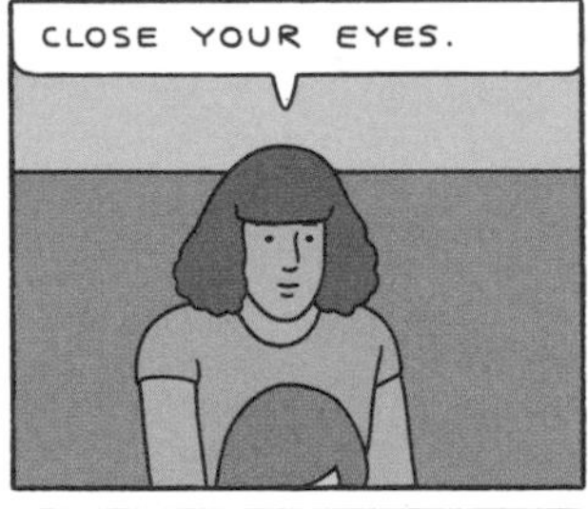
CLOSE YOUR EYES.

PLACE YOUR HANDS IN A COMFORTABLE POSITION.

NOW TAKE A DEEP BREATH.
AND LET IT OUT SLOWLY.
DO THAT AGAIN.
GOOD.
JUST FOCUS ON YOUR BREATHING.
CAN YOU FEEL IT TRAVEL DOWN TO YOUR FEET?
TO THE ENDS OF YOUR FINGERS?
SLOW AND DEEP.
KEEP BREATHING. LET YOUR SHOULDERS DROP.
FEEL YOURSELF SINK BACK WITH EACH BREATH OUT.
OK. NOW ALLOW A PLACE TO COME TO MIND.
A PLACE WHERE YOU CAN FEEL SAFE AND PEACEFUL.
IT CAN BE REAL OR IMAGINARY.
ALLOW YOURSELF TO STEP FORWARD.

LOOK TO YOUR RIGHT.
NOW LOOK TO YOUR LEFT.
ALLOW YOURSELF TO FEEL THE WEATHER. OBSERVE THE COLORS.
NOW WALK TO THE PLACE WHERE YOU WANT TO GO. THE PLACE WHERE YOU WILL FEEL SAFE AND CALM.
ENTER THE PLACE, WHATEVER IT MAY BE.
GO TO THE PLACE WHERE YOU CAN BE AT PEACE.
AND REST.
BREATHE IN AND OUT.
SLOW AND FULL.
AND BE AT PEACE.
YOU ARE AT PEACE.

YOU ARE AT PEACE.
OPEN YOUR EYES WHENEVER YOU FEEL COMFORTABLE.
UM...
HOW DO YOU FEEL?
I STILL DON'T KNOW WHAT TO DO.
FUCK. I DON'T KNOW WHAT TO DO...
AH, FUCK.
GOD FUCKING DAMMIT. I WANT IT TO STOP.
HEY.
HEY.
I WANT IT TO STOP!
HEY.
I WANT IT TO STOP!
HEY.
STOP.

SHH...

AHH!

OH MY GOD.

I THINK I WANT TO BE ALONE RIGHT NOW.

ARE YOU SURE? I CAN SPEND THE NIGHT IF YOU NEED ME TO.

I'M SORRY. I CAN'T SIT HERE WITH YOU RIGHT NOW.

I REALLY WANT TO BE ALONE.

ALL RIGHT.

WILL YOU CALL ME TOMORROW?

YOU'RE NOT GOING TO DO ANYTHING TONIGHT, ARE YOU?

NO.

PLEASE CALL ME IF YOU NEED ME AND I'LL COME BACK.
THANKS.
ANNA!
ANNA!

Old Style

MAIL CALL.

THANKS, TERRY.

THE MAYOR'S CONFERENCE WAS CONFIRMED FOR TWO THIRTY THIS AFTERNOON.

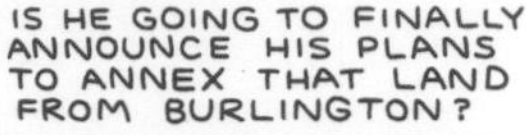
IS HE GOING TO FINALLY ANNOUNCE HIS PLANS TO ANNEX THAT LAND FROM BURLINGTON?

THAT'S THE BUZZ. FROM BACHELOR'S GROVE CEMETERY DOWN TO GLEN GOLF COURSE.

GREAT. WE'LL LEAD WITH THAT TOMORROW.

COFFEE?

SURE.

GOOD MORNING, MONA.

HEY, GREG. DID YOU TRY THE SHORTBREAD? GOES GREAT WITH YOUR COFFEE THERE.

MY DENTIST TOLD ME I NEED SIX CAVITIES FILLED, A ROOT CANAL, AND A DEEP CLEANING.

THANKS, BUT I SHOULDN'T.

THESE STUPID DENTISTS ARE NOW TELLING ME TO CUT OUT SWEETS COMPLETELY.

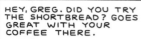

YIKES.

SO I DECIDED TO GET A SECOND OPINION, AND THIS NEW DENTIST IS TELLING ME I'M GETTING RIPPED OFF, AND THAT I ONLY HAVE ONE MINOR CAVITY!
YEA?

WHEN I TELL THIS TO MY FIRST DENTIST, HE TELLS ME THAT THIS OTHER DENTIST HAS BEEN POACHING HIS BUSINESS FOR YEARS THE SAME WAY.

HE SAID THIS GUY NEGLECTS HIS PATIENT'S TEETH UNTIL THEY'RE SO BAD THEY NEED MAJOR, EXPENSIVE SURGERY. THAT'S HIS GAME.

REALLY?

NOW I DON'T KNOW WHAT THE HELL TO DO. I'VE HAD EIGHT DENTIST APPOINTMENTS IN THE PAST YEAR. THESE GUYS ARE TAKING ME FOR A RIDE.

WHAT'S THAT?

I DON'T KNOW. RETURN ADDRESS IS FROM ILLINOIS.
THAT'S WEIRD.

DO WE EVEN HAVE A VHS PLAYER ANYMORE?

MM. YEA. I THINK SO. LET'S TAKE A LOOK IN THE BACK.

HERE WE GO.
RED TO RED... WHITE TO WHITE...
LOOK AT THAT!
WHAT?
MY KID'S BARNEY TAPE. JESUS! I TURNED MY HOUSE UPSIDE DOWN LOOKING FOR THIS.
AUX
HM. TRY "CHANNEL."
FRONT
STUPID THING.
CHANNEL THREE MAYBE?
NOPE.
WAIT! THERE'S SOMETHING.

...I SUPPOSE WE SHOULD CALL THE POLICE.

YES, HELLO. THIS IS MONA NEWMAN FROM THE STANDARD JOURNAL.

WE JUST RECEIVED A TAPE AT OUR OFFICE THAT APPEARS TO SHOW A YOUNG WOMAN BEING MURDERED.

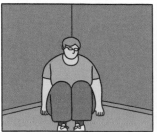

I HAVE NO IDEA.

YES, THEY CAN MEET US HERE.

THERE'S A RETURN ADDRESS ON THE PACK-AGE. DO YOU WANT IT?

FOUR. NINE. THREE. ONE. NORTH. HARDING. STREET. ILLINOIS.

IT JUST SAYS ILLINOIS.

THANK YOU. BYE NOW.

TIMMY YANCEY. TWENTY-THREE YEARS OLD.

HE'S BEEN RENTING THE UPSTAIRS APARTMENT SINCE MAY OF 2016.

OK. WHAT CAN YOU TELL ME ABOUT HIM?

WELL, I DIDN'T SEE HIM THAT MUCH.

I DON'T THINK HE HAD A JOB. THE RENT CHECKS CAME FROM HIS MOTHER.

I HEARD HIM WALK-ING AROUND A LOT. ONE TIME I DID ASK HIM TO TURN HIS VIDEO GAMES DOWN, BUT HE DIDN'T DO IT.

I MET HIS MOTHER. SHE WAS THE ONLY ONE WHO HELPED HIM MOVE IN. IT WAS HIS FIRST TIME LEAVING HOME. I REMEMBER THAT.

CAN YOU REMEMBER ANYTHING UNUSUAL ABOUT HIS TIME LEASING THE APARTMENT? ANY-THING THAT STANDS OUT?

YEA, YOU KNOW, I'VE BEEN THINKING ABOUT IT. MAYBE TWO MONTHS AGO I HEARD PEOPLE TALKING UPSTAIRS AT NIGHT. LIKE TWO IN THE MORNING.

I DON'T KNOW IF THAT MEANS ANYTHING. I JUST THOUGHT IT WAS STRANGE BECAUSE HE NEVER REALLY HAD COMPANY OVER.

COULD YOU HEAR WHAT THEY WERE SAYING?

NO. BUT THERE WERE AT LEAST THREE MALE VOICES.

AND WHAT ABOUT THE PAST MONTH? NOTICE ANYTHING UNUSUAL?

MICHAEL?
NO. I CAN'T SAY THAT I HAVE.
EXCUSE ME FOR A MOMENT.
TAKE YOUR TIME.
MAY I KEEP THIS LEASE AGREEMENT?
CERTAINLY. I'M HERE TO HELP.

THIS WAS PHOTOGRAPH-
ED ALREADY?
YEP.

HEY, CALVIN. COME LOOK AT THIS.
I, UH.
THIS JUST HAPPENED IN ILLINOIS. HAVE YOU SEEN THIS?
I HAVE TO GO HOME.
WHAT'S WRONG, CAL?
HEY!
TELL SERGEANT SMITH IT'S AN EMERGENCY. I'LL EXPLAIN LATER!
I GOTTA GO!
TEDDY!
CALVIN? WHAT'S WRONG?
WHAT'S WRONG?

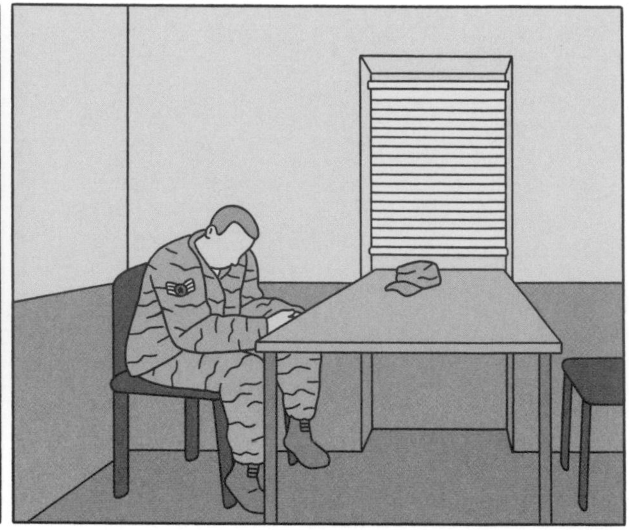

HOW ARE YOU DOING, MR. WROBEL?

I'M ALL RIGHT.

THE DETECTIVES JUST GOT HERE BY RED EYE FROM CHICAGO.

HOW'S TEDDY?

HE'S STILL SHAKEN UP.

THEY'RE TRYING TO TALK TO HIM RIGHT NOW.

THANKS FOR COMING DOWN HERE WITH US.

I DIDN'T WANT TO BE THE ONE TO BREAK IT TO HIM IF WE EVER GOT THE BAD NEWS ABOUT SABRINA.

I TRIED TO PREPARE MYSELF. BUT NOT FOR THIS.

MAN...

-SNF-

LET'S TRY TO GO OVER WHAT HAPPENED IN YOUR HOUSE. WHEN YOUR NEIGHBORS CALLED NINE-ONE-ONE, THEY THOUGHT SOMEONE WAS BEING KILLED OVER THERE.

I TOLD TEDDY WHAT HAPPENED, AND HE LOST HIS MIND.

I TRIED TO SUBDUE HIM, AND HE STRUGGLED AGAINST ME. WE BOUNCED AROUND MY LIVING ROOM AND KNOCKED THE TELEVIS-ION OFF THE WALL.

WERE YOU IN FEAR THAT HE WAS GOING TO HARM YOU?

NO, NO. I JUST DIDN'T KNOW WHAT HE WAS CAPABLE OF IN THAT MOMENT. HE WAS HYS-TERICAL, LIKE HE WAS POSSESSED.

WHAT MY NEIGHBORS HEARD WAS PROBABLY TEDDY SCREAMING "NO!"

I SEE. DID YOU FEEL THAT HE WAS CAPABLE OF HARMING HIMSELF?

I DON'T KNOW. LIKE I SAID, HE WAS JUST GOING NUTS.

WELL, I NEED TO ASK YOU IF YOU THINK HE IS A SUICIDE RISK? HAS HE SAID ANYTHING DISCONCERTING?
POLI

NO, NOTHING LIKE THAT.
ROBEL
U.S.

YOU'RE SURE ABOUT THAT?

YEA.

DO YOU STILL FEEL COMFORTABLE LETTING HIM STAY WITH YOU?

YEA, I THINK SO. WHATEVER HE WANTS TO DO.

OK. ONE OF THE DETEC-TIVES WANTS TO TALK TO YOU. SIT TIGHT.

WHATEVER YOU WANT.

CALVIN?

I'M DETECTIVE CRAIG.

HOW'S TEDDY?

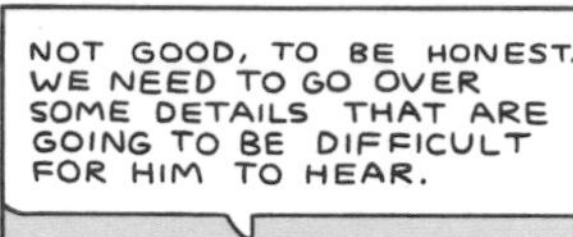
NOT GOOD, TO BE HONEST. WE NEED TO GO OVER SOME DETAILS THAT ARE GOING TO BE DIFFICULT FOR HIM TO HEAR.

IS THERE REALLY A TAPE OF IT?

I'M AFRAID SO. MORE THAN A FEW, ACTUALLY.

JESUS CHRIST.

WE'RE TRYING OUR BEST TO SECURE THEM ALL. HE SENT OUT SEVERAL TO NEWS OUTLETS ALL OVER THE COUNTRY, A FEW TO LOCAL POLITICIANS, ONE TO A SPORTSCASTER IN CHICAGO.

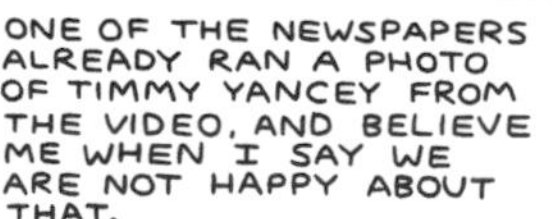
ONE OF THE NEWSPAPERS ALREADY RAN A PHOTO OF TIMMY YANCEY FROM THE VIDEO, AND BELIEVE ME WHEN I SAY WE ARE NOT HAPPY ABOUT THAT.

WE'RE DESPERATELY TRYING TO KEEP THIS VIDEO FROM LEAKING ONTO THE INTERNET, FOR THE SAKE OF TEDDY AND THE VICTIM'S FAMILY.

YEA.

HOW LONG HAS MR. KING BEEN STAYING WITH YOU?
ABOUT THREE WEEKS.
HOW'S HE BEEN HANDLING EVERYTHING?

WE DON'T TALK MUCH. HE STAYS IN HIS ROOM MOST OF THE TIME. SLEEPS A LOT. DOESN'T EAT ENOUGH, BUT I FORCE HIM.

DOESN'T TALK ON THE PHONE? SURF THE INTERNET?

NO.

HAS HE TALKED TO HIS FAMILY AT ALL? SABRINA'S FAMILY?
I DON'T THINK SO. I HAVE THE ONLY PHONE.
HAS HE SAID ANYTHING ABOUT HIS REASONS FOR LEAVING CHICAGO?

NO.
WHY DO YOU THINK HE DECIDED TO STAY WITH YOU?

I DON'T KNOW. MAYBE HE JUST WANTED TO STAY WITH SOMEONE HE'S NOT THAT CLOSE WITH. LIKE A FRESH START.

THAT'S NOT THE RIGHT WAY TO SAY IT. I DON'T KNOW. HE JUST WANTS TO NOT EXIST, AT LEAST FOR NOW, IT SEEMS.

HAS HE SAID ANYTHING ABOUT HIS RELATIONSHIP WITH SABRINA UP TO THE POINT OF HER ABDUCTION?

NOT MUCH, BUT ONLY GOOD THINGS. I THINK HE REALLY LOVED HER.

RIGHT.
WHERE DID IT HAPPEN?

TIMMY YANCEY LIVED ONE BLOCK OVER FROM SABRINA'S APARTMENT, BELIEVE IT OR NOT.

ARE YOU FUCKING KIDDING ME?

AND IT WAS ONE GUY?

ONE PERSON THAT WE KNOW OF, OBVIOUSLY. WE'RE LOOKING INTO IT.

WE'RE TRYING TO FINISH UP WITH TEDDY FOR THE NIGHT. HE'S BEEN THROUGH ENOUGH TOR-TURE. HE'LL BE READY TO GO HOME WITH YOU IN AN HOUR OR SO. IS THAT OK?

YES.

WE'LL BE STAYING IN TOWN TOMORROW. WE MAY WANT TO TALK TO HIM AGAIN. HERE'S MY CARD IF YOU NEED TO REACH ME.

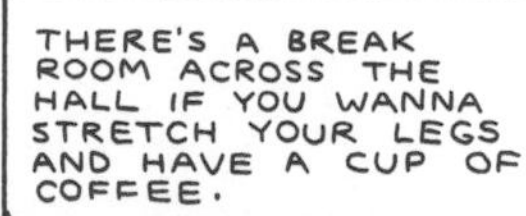

THERE'S A BREAK ROOM ACROSS THE HALL IF YOU WANNA STRETCH YOUR LEGS AND HAVE A CUP OF COFFEE.

I'LL JUST WAIT HERE.

HEY, JACKIE. HOW ARE YOU?

ME? I'M NOT GOOD.

I CAN'T TALK ABOUT IT RIGHT NOW. I'LL EX-PLAIN LATER.

IS CICI THERE? I NEED TO TALK TO HER.

OH, RIGHT. I'M SORRY. I DIDN'T REALIZE HOW LATE IT WAS.

IS SHE SAFE? SHE'S AT HOME WITH YOU RIGHT NOW?

I WAS JUST CHECKING.

OK. BYE NOW.

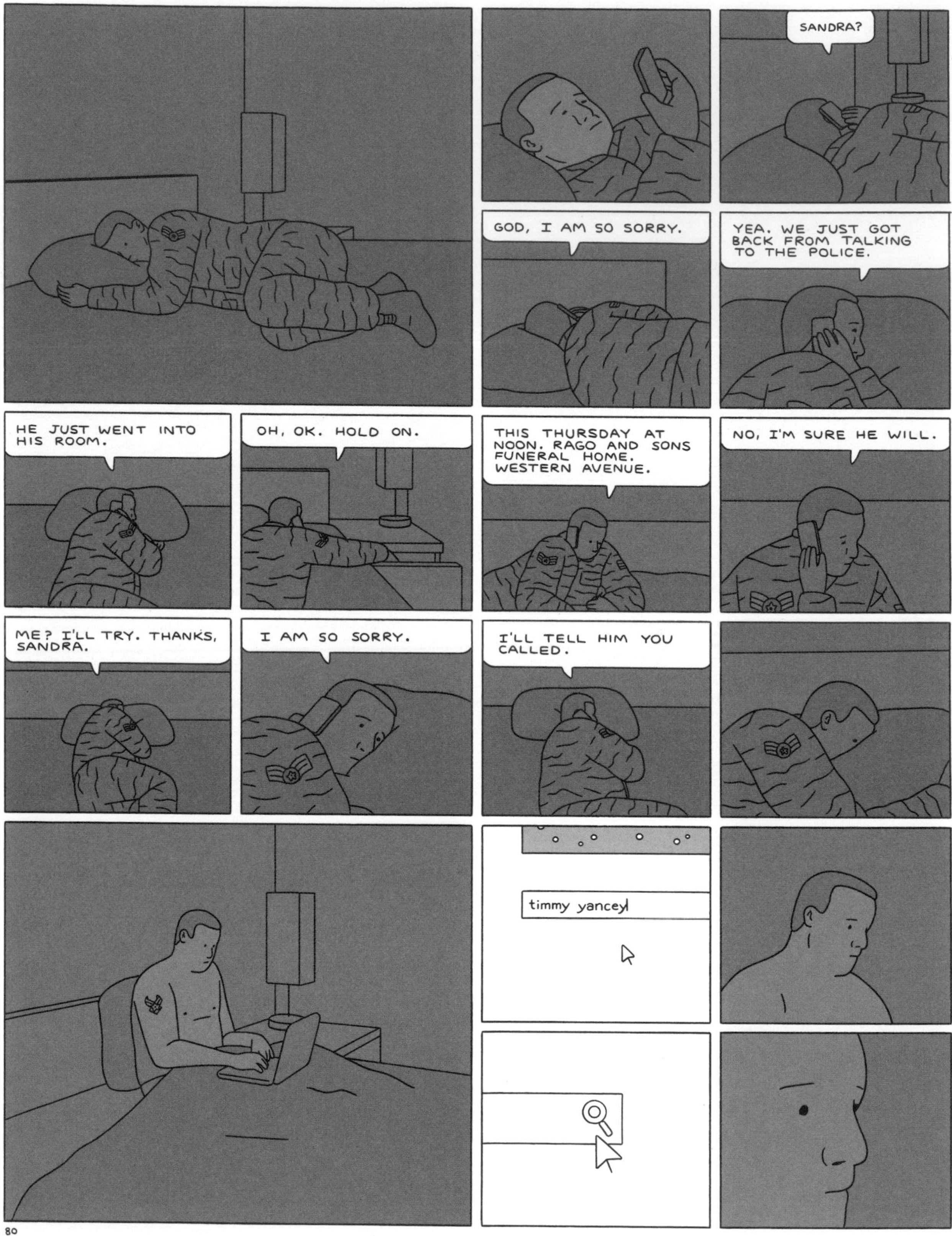
SANDRA?
GOD, I AM SO SORRY.
YEA. WE JUST GOT BACK FROM TALKING TO THE POLICE.
HE JUST WENT INTO HIS ROOM.
OH, OK. HOLD ON.
THIS THURSDAY AT NOON. RAGO AND SONS FUNERAL HOME. WESTERN AVENUE.
NO, I'M SURE HE WILL.
ME? I'LL TRY. THANKS, SANDRA.
I AM SO SORRY.
I'LL TELL HIM YOU CALLED.
timmy yancey

Most Popular

October 2, 2017, 11:11 PM

What we know about Timmy Yancey

653 Comments / 316 Tweets / Share

2 Lost a significant amount of weight from the last time his parents saw him to his time of death. Possibly up to forty pounds.

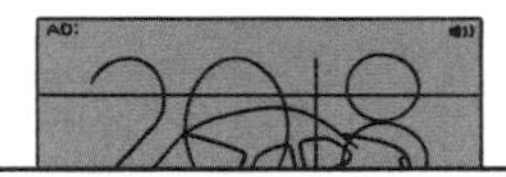

4 Yancey was active on various message boards ranging from body-building and men's rights to theoretical physics and organic farming. Apparently, he was banned from several online groups for dominating the discussions with long, vitriolic rants.

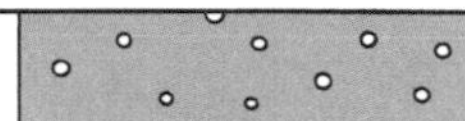

have already obtained more than thirty tapes, and are imploring anyone that has received anything suspicious in the mail to contact authorities immediately.

SHOW COMMENTS

ities immediately.

HIDE COMMENTS

SOBOB44 1:37 AM

I NEED to see this.

101 / REPLY

JIMBEE866 1:37 AM

link?

79 / REPLY

Trending Now

#TimmyYancey
#Playoffs
#SalmonRecall
#SabrinaGallo
#TheAvengers

sabrina gallo

The victim, twenty-seven-year old Chicago native Sabrina Ga

no apparent connection t
been living in her apart
boyfriend since August o
planned to leave Chicago
working as a volunteer a
sparked by her passion fo

unable to find a clearly marked suicide note, but what seems to be his last message board post, appearing hours before his estimated time of death, is a list of his fifty favorite movies, ending with the sign-off "Bye for now."

Most Discussed:

what happens next will shock you

You don't want to know what this economist predicts for 2018

Teen surprises mom and toddler with good deed at mall

A Northwest-Indiana teen is being praised on social media after his random act of kindness went viral.

It all began when Beth Russell, a resident of Portage, was birthday shopping with her youngest daughter, Paige.

As the two-year-old scanned the aisles of toys, her eyes fixed on a blonde doll, the last one on the shelf.

Before she could show her mom the doll, a young man walked over and asked if it was her favorite. She told the stranger that her birthday was approaching, and that she really loved the doll.

The teen laughed, grabbed the doll and left the aisle.

A few minutes later, the young man returned to the aisle with a bag under his arm. He handed Paige's mom a receipt, took the doll out of the bag and wished Paige a happy birthday.

Russell was at a loss for words. After a moment, she managed to thank him for the gift. The teen nodded, smiled and walked off. Before he was out of sight, Russell ushered him back to take a photo with Paige.

That night, Russell shared the story with her friends on Facebook, posting the photo of Paige with the young man, hoping that someone would be able to identify him.

After thousands of shares, someone recognized the teen as Centell Rodgers III, a senior football player at Horace Mann High School.

Russell thanked him again, for showing her daughter that hope is not lost on society as a whole.

Her hope is that sharing this story will inspire others to do good in the community.

"This extraordinary young man has taught Paige a meaningful life lesson. I'm so grateful for that."

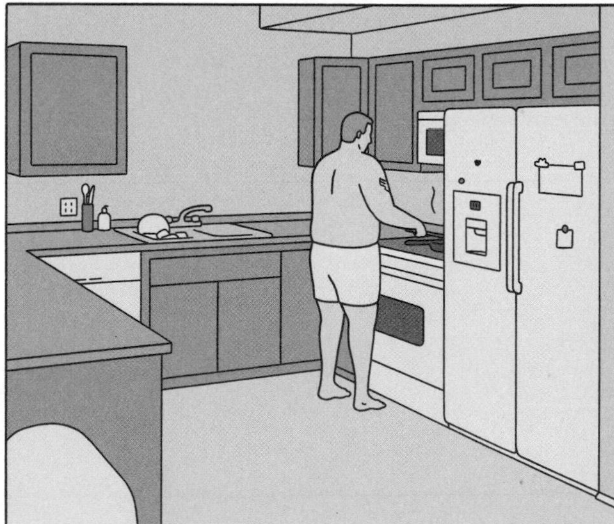

SERGEANT SMITH? IT'S CALVIN.

DID YOU SEE IT ON THE NEWS?

YEA.

HE'S HERE. HE'S OK I GUESS.

DID DAHLMAN TALK TO YOU LAST NIGHT?

I'M SORRY FOR RUNNING OUT LIKE THAT.

MM.

I APPRECIATE THAT.

DO YOU THINK IT WOULD BE ALL RIGHT IF I STAY-ED HOME WITH TEDDY TONIGHT? I'M WORRIED ABOUT LEAVING HIM ALONE.

THANKS FOR BEING COOL ABOUT IT.

I'LL KEEP YOU POSTED.

TEDDY?

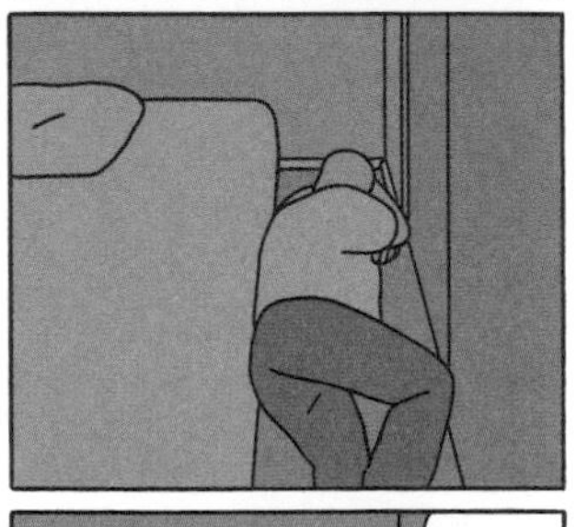

ARE YOU OK?

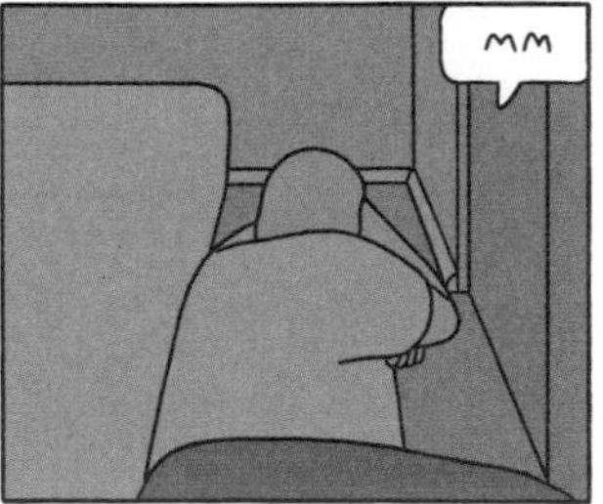
MM

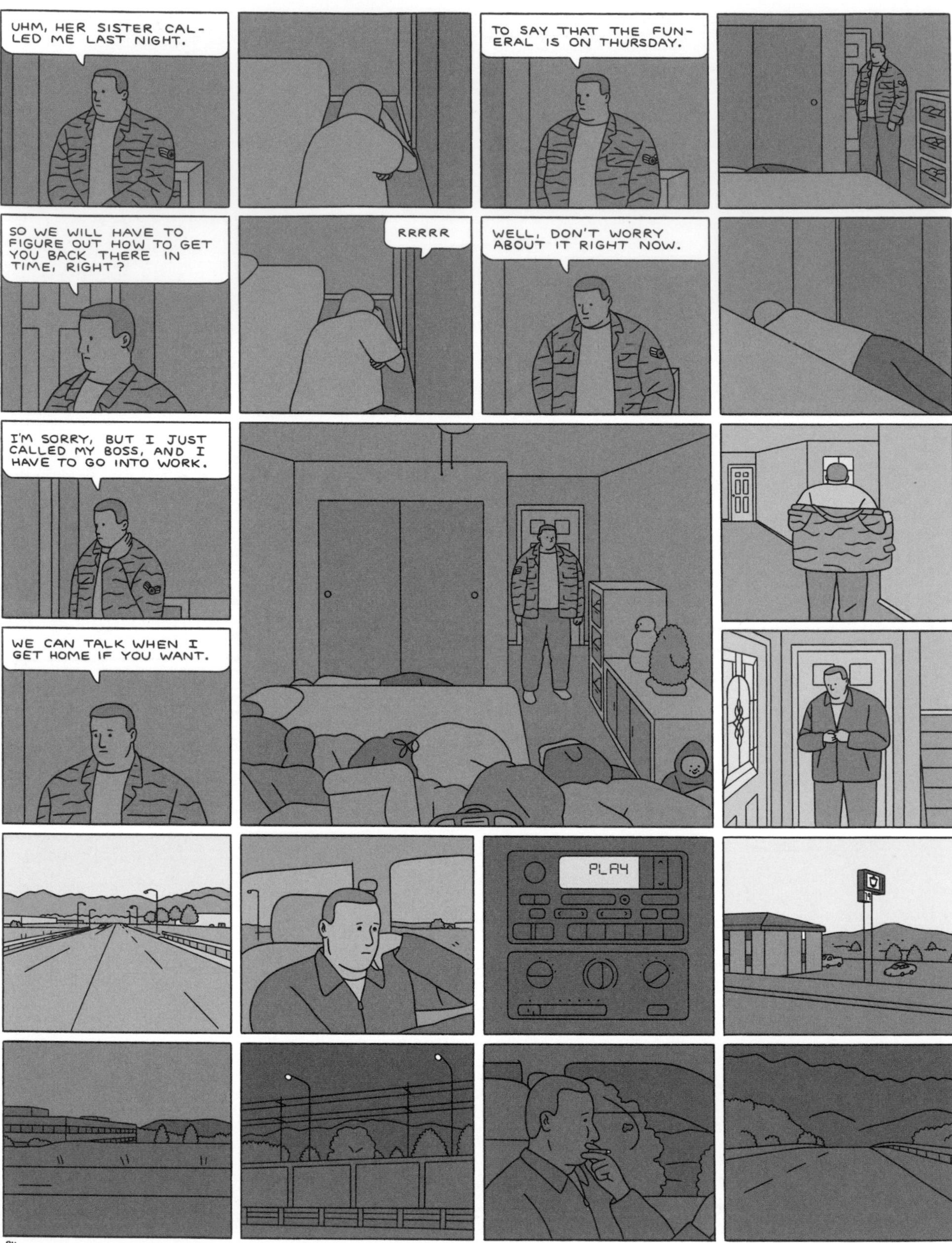
UHM, HER SISTER CALLED ME LAST NIGHT.
TO SAY THAT THE FUNERAL IS ON THURSDAY.
SO WE WILL HAVE TO FIGURE OUT HOW TO GET YOU BACK THERE IN TIME, RIGHT?
RRRRR
WELL, DON'T WORRY ABOUT IT RIGHT NOW.
I'M SORRY, BUT I JUST CALLED MY BOSS, AND I HAVE TO GO INTO WORK.
WE CAN TALK WHEN I GET HOME IF YOU WANT.
PLAY

HI. SORRY...
HM?
DO YOU HAVE A PUBLIC RESTROOM?
OK - GO STRAIGHT AHEAD. GO THROUGH THE SWING - ING DOORS INTO THE LOADING DOCK. GO ALL THE WAY TO THE BACK AND MAKE A LEFT. GO UP THE STAIRS, INTO THE EMPLOYEE BREAK-ROOM AND IT'S THERE.
ARE YOU SURE IT'S OK?
SURE! DO YOU THINK YOU CAN HANDLE THAT?
HAHA
HA, I'LL TRY. THANKS A LOT.

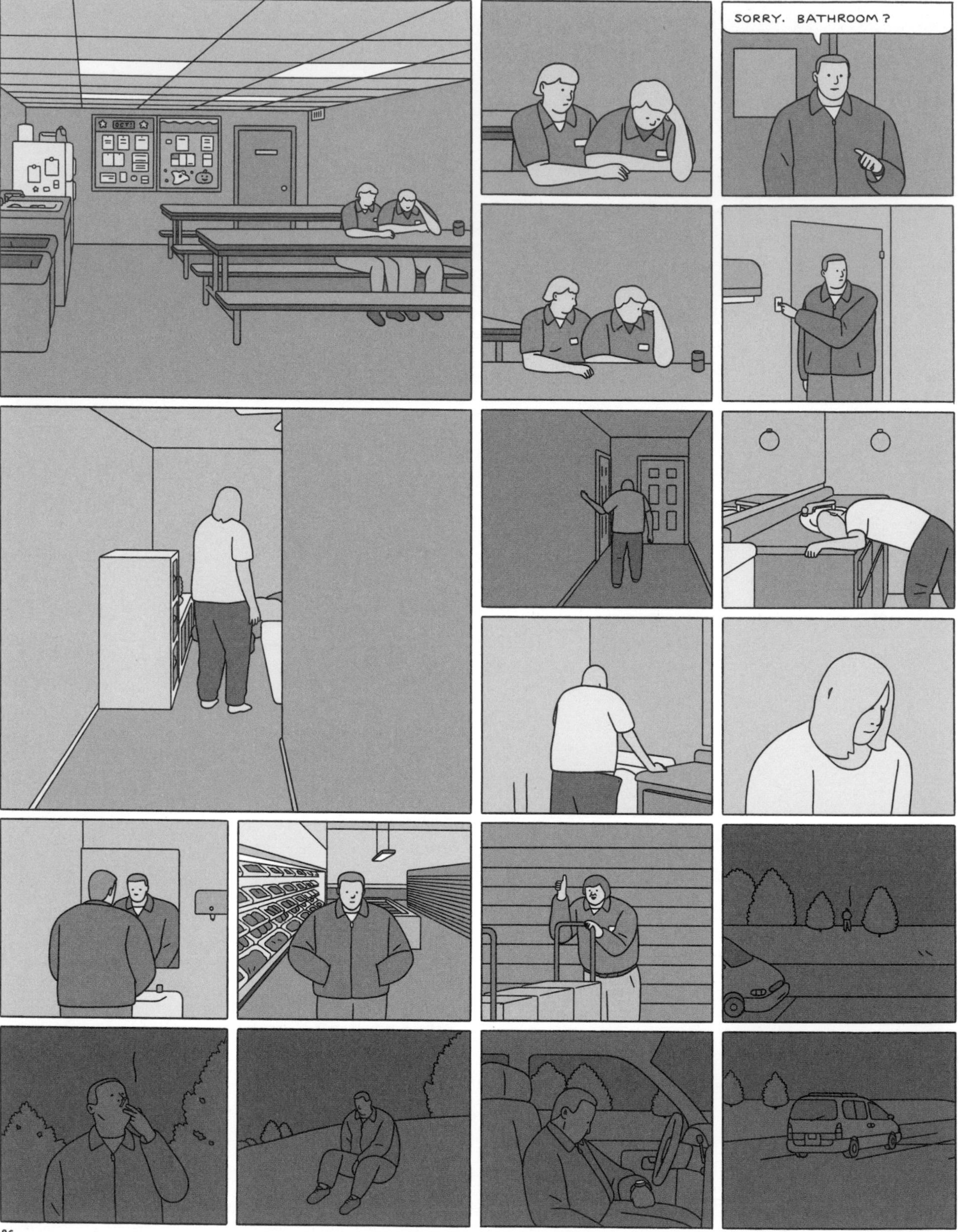
SORRY. BATHROOM?

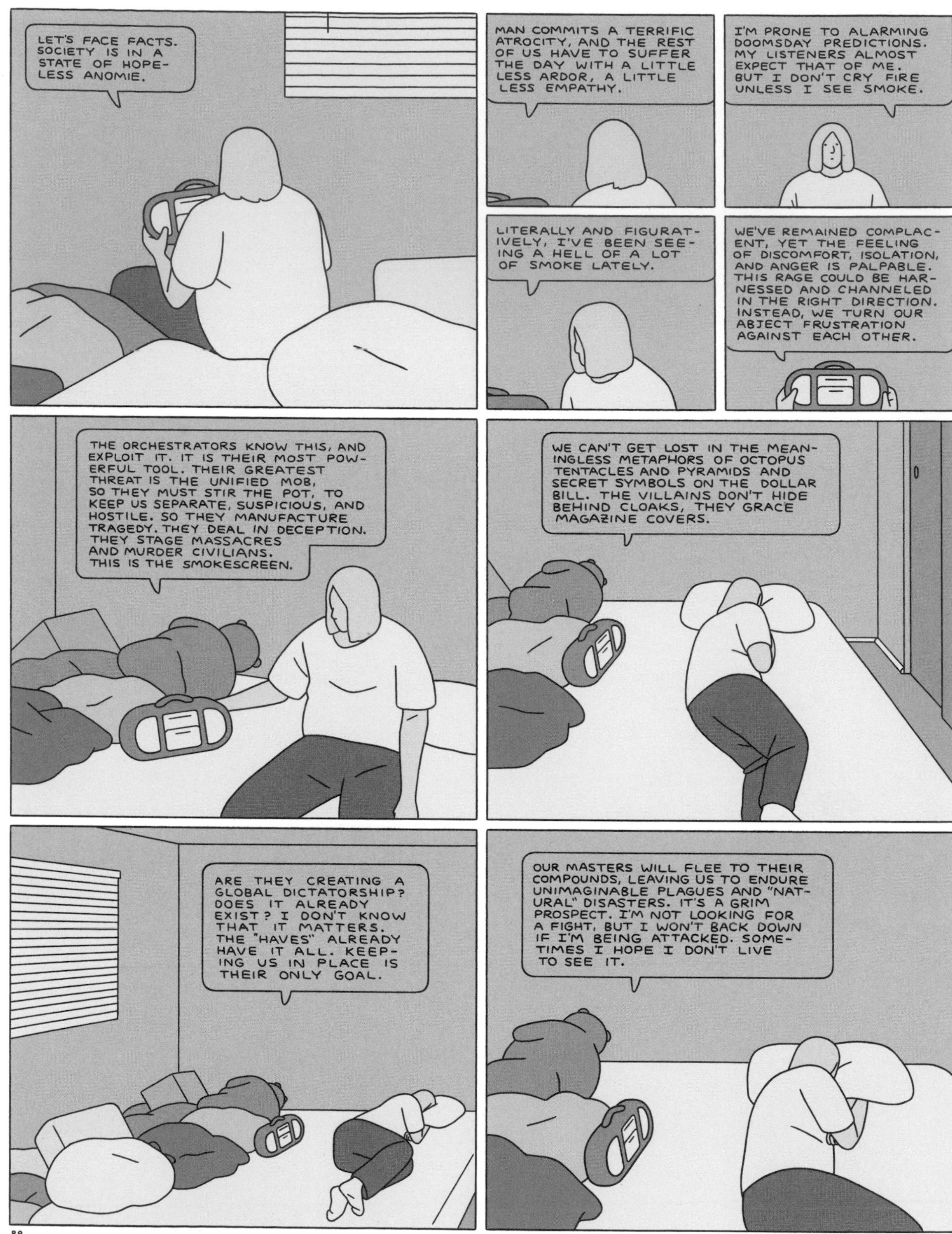
LET'S FACE FACTS. SOCIETY IS IN A STATE OF HOPELESS ANOMIE.
MAN COMMITS A TERRIFIC ATROCITY, AND THE REST OF US HAVE TO SUFFER THE DAY WITH A LITTLE LESS ARDOR, A LITTLE LESS EMPATHY.
I'M PRONE TO ALARMING DOOMSDAY PREDICTIONS. MY LISTENERS ALMOST EXPECT THAT OF ME. BUT I DON'T CRY FIRE UNLESS I SEE SMOKE.
LITERALLY AND FIGURATIVELY, I'VE BEEN SEEING A HELL OF A LOT OF SMOKE LATELY.
WE'VE REMAINED COMPLACENT, YET THE FEELING OF DISCOMFORT, ISOLATION, AND ANGER IS PALPABLE. THIS RAGE COULD BE HARNESSED AND CHANNELED IN THE RIGHT DIRECTION. INSTEAD, WE TURN OUR ABJECT FRUSTRATION AGAINST EACH OTHER.
THE ORCHESTRATORS KNOW THIS, AND EXPLOIT IT. IT IS THEIR MOST POWERFUL TOOL. THEIR GREATEST THREAT IS THE UNIFIED MOB, SO THEY MUST STIR THE POT, TO KEEP US SEPARATE, SUSPICIOUS, AND HOSTILE. SO THEY MANUFACTURE TRAGEDY. THEY DEAL IN DECEPTION. THEY STAGE MASSACRES AND MURDER CIVILIANS. THIS IS THE SMOKESCREEN.
WE CAN'T GET LOST IN THE MEANINGLESS METAPHORS OF OCTOPUS TENTACLES AND PYRAMIDS AND SECRET SYMBOLS ON THE DOLLAR BILL. THE VILLAINS DON'T HIDE BEHIND CLOAKS, THEY GRACE MAGAZINE COVERS.
ARE THEY CREATING A GLOBAL DICTATORSHIP? DOES IT ALREADY EXIST? I DON'T KNOW THAT IT MATTERS. THE "HAVES" ALREADY HAVE IT ALL. KEEPING US IN PLACE IS THEIR ONLY GOAL.
OUR MASTERS WILL FLEE TO THEIR COMPOUNDS, LEAVING US TO ENDURE UNIMAGINABLE PLAGUES AND "NATURAL" DISASTERS. IT'S A GRIM PROSPECT. I'M NOT LOOKING FOR A FIGHT, BUT I WON'T BACK DOWN IF I'M BEING ATTACKED. SOMETIMES I HOPE I DON'T LIVE TO SEE IT.

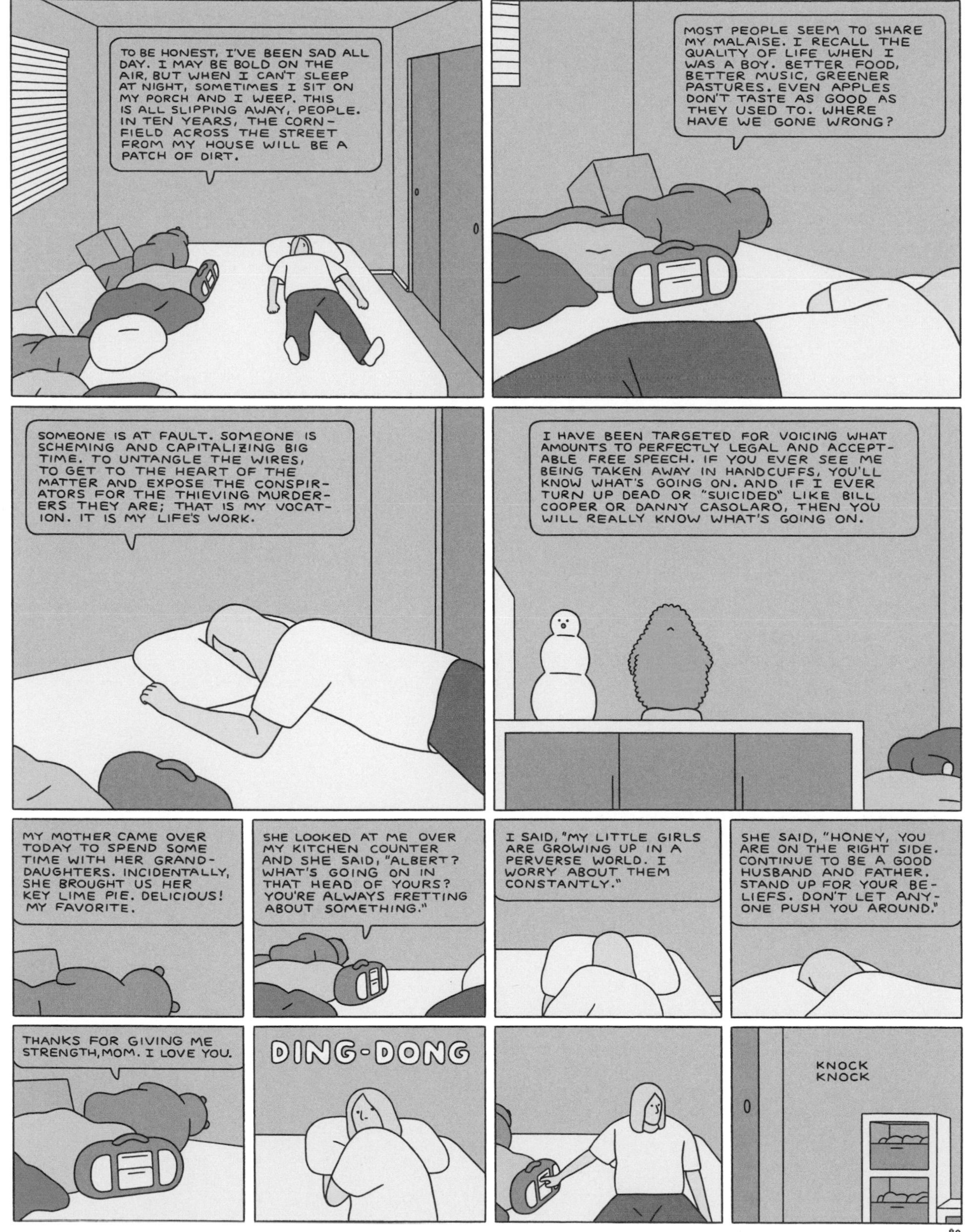
TO BE HONEST, I'VE BEEN SAD ALL DAY. I MAY BE BOLD ON THE AIR, BUT WHEN I CAN'T SLEEP AT NIGHT, SOMETIMES I SIT ON MY PORCH AND I WEEP. THIS IS ALL SLIPPING AWAY, PEOPLE. IN TEN YEARS, THE CORN-FIELD ACROSS THE STREET FROM MY HOUSE WILL BE A PATCH OF DIRT.
MOST PEOPLE SEEM TO SHARE MY MALAISE. I RECALL THE QUALITY OF LIFE WHEN I WAS A BOY. BETTER FOOD, BETTER MUSIC, GREENER PASTURES. EVEN APPLES DON'T TASTE AS GOOD AS THEY USED TO. WHERE HAVE WE GONE WRONG?
SOMEONE IS AT FAULT. SOMEONE IS SCHEMING AND CAPITALIZING BIG TIME. TO UNTANGLE THE WIRES, TO GET TO THE HEART OF THE MATTER AND EXPOSE THE CONSPIR-ATORS FOR THE THIEVING MURDER-ERS THEY ARE; THAT IS MY VOCAT-ION. IT IS MY LIFE'S WORK.
I HAVE BEEN TARGETED FOR VOICING WHAT AMOUNTS TO PERFECTLY LEGAL AND ACCEPT-ABLE FREE SPEECH. IF YOU EVER SEE ME BEING TAKEN AWAY IN HANDCUFFS, YOU'LL KNOW WHAT'S GOING ON. AND IF I EVER TURN UP DEAD OR "SUICIDED" LIKE BILL COOPER OR DANNY CASOLARO, THEN YOU WILL REALLY KNOW WHAT'S GOING ON.
MY MOTHER CAME OVER TODAY TO SPEND SOME TIME WITH HER GRAND-DAUGHTERS. INCIDENTALLY, SHE BROUGHT US HER KEY LIME PIE. DELICIOUS! MY FAVORITE.
SHE LOOKED AT ME OVER MY KITCHEN COUNTER AND SHE SAID, "ALBERT? WHAT'S GOING ON IN THAT HEAD OF YOURS? YOU'RE ALWAYS FRETTING ABOUT SOMETHING."
I SAID, "MY LITTLE GIRLS ARE GROWING UP IN A PERVERSE WORLD. I WORRY ABOUT THEM CONSTANTLY."
SHE SAID, "HONEY, YOU ARE ON THE RIGHT SIDE. CONTINUE TO BE A GOOD HUSBAND AND FATHER. STAND UP FOR YOUR BE-LIEFS. DON'T LET ANY-ONE PUSH YOU AROUND."
THANKS FOR GIVING ME STRENGTH, MOM. I LOVE YOU.
DING-DONG
KNOCK KNOCK

DING-DONG
HELLO?

TEDDY? I'M COMING IN.
HOW ARE YOU DOING?
DID YOU DECIDE IF YOU WANT TO GO BACK FOR THE SERVICE?
I'M NOT GOING.
-SNF-

Old Style
RESTAURANT
PLAN A PARTY
OPEN TIL 4AM
KARAOKE
AZA
Cafe
onDo
Cafe

THE FOLLOWING PREVIEW IS FOR A MOTION PICTURE
THAT HAS BEEN RATED
BY THE MOTION PICTURE ASSOCIATION OF AMERICA
THE FILM ADVERTISED HAS BEEN RATED
G
GENERAL AUDIENCES
All Ages Admitted

THANKS.

HEY EVERYBODY.

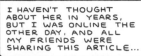

THIS WILL BE A SHORT ONE.

UM, WHEN I WAS IN JUNIOR HIGH SCHOOL, I KNEW THIS GIRL NAMED MICHELLE.

I HAVEN'T THOUGHT ABOUT HER IN YEARS, BUT I WAS ONLINE THE OTHER DAY, AND ALL MY FRIENDS WERE SHARING THIS ARTICLE...

Corner ◇ Cafe

SORRY, I DIDN'T KNOW THIS THING WAS HAPPENING.

IT'S OK.

SHOULD WE STAY OR GO?

NO, THIS IS FINE.

I DON'T KNOW WHAT I WOULD SAY TO HER IF I SAW HER AGAIN.

I GUESS I SHOULD REACH OUT.

ANYWAY, SORRY FOR RAMBLING. THANK YOU FOR LISTENING.

GREAT.

OK, THANK YOU EVERY-ONE FOR COMING.

THE FIRST WEDNESDAY OF EVERY MONTH WE GATHER HERE TO SHARE STORIES.

THERE ARE NO GUIDE-LINES. YOU CAN BE SAD, FUNNY. YOU CAN CON-FESS YOUR DEEPEST, DARKEST SECRETS.

I WANTED TO CREATE AN EVENT WHERE ANY-ONE CAN SHOW UP AND HAVE A PLATFORM. I THINK WE SPEND TOO MUCH TIME IN ISOLATION.

THIS IS A CHANCE FOR REGULAR PEOPLE LIKE US TO SHARE OUR THOUGHTS. I THINK THIS IS A HEALTHY OUTLET. AT LEAST FOR ME. HA HA.

OK. SO OUR NEXT PRESENTER IS PETE. PETE?

THANKS!

MY BOSS IS A COMPLETE ASSHOLE.

ALMOST EVERY DAY HE YELLS AT ME FOR THINGS OTHER PEOPLE SHOULD BE DOING.

"IT'S NOT MY RESPON-SIBILITY." I WANT TO SCREAM AT HIM. I DIDN'T SIGN UP FOR THIS.

BUT LIKE, I THINK HE'S CRAZY, LIKE, LITERALLY MENTALLY ILL OR SOMETHING.

I'M PRETTY WELL-LIKED AT MY JOB. I'M KIND OF THE COMIC RELIEF.

NO, THANKS. I'M JUST GONNA GO HOME.

I'M GONNA GO.

ARE YOU SURE? CAN I COME WITH YOU?

OK. I LOVE YOU.

LOVE YOU TOO.

WOW!
HAHA
WANNA MAKE A RUN FOR IT ?
HA!
WHOA!
DAHLMAN! THINK FAST!
HEY!
I'LL GET HIM!
DIE!
HAHA
WHOA, COLD! I GIVE UP!
SEE YA LATER.
GET HOME SAFE!
LET'S CUT THROUGH THIS FIELD.
DID YOU HEAR ABOUT WHAT HAPPENED IN OMAHA TODAY ?
MAN, I DON'T EVEN WANT TO KNOW ABOUT IT.

I'M GOING THROUGH THIS PHASE WHERE I JUST FEEL LIKE "I DON'T CARE HOW MANY PEOPLE WERE SHOT TO-DAY. I CAN'T TAKE IT."

YOU DON'T FOLLOW THE NEWS AT ALL?

NOT SINCE EVERYTHING HAPPENED.

WHAT'S GOING ON WITH TEDDY?

WE HAVE OUR ROUTINE. I LEAVE FOOD AT HIS BEDROOM DOOR WHEN I GET HOME AT NIGHT. USUALLY CHEESEBURGERS. AS FAR AS I CAN TELL, HE SLEEPS A LOT AND TAKES WALKS SOMETIMES.

SOUNDS LIKE A PRETTY GOOD DEAL.

I DIDN'T MEAN IT LIKE THAT.

DUDE, HIS GIRLFRIEND WAS MURDERED.

I KNOW, I'M SORRY. I JUST MEAN HE'S LUCKY TO HAVE YOU TAKING CARE OF HIM.

YEA, WELL, HE'S GET-TING THROUGH IT SOMEHOW.

DID THE MEDIA EVER CONTACT YOU THROUGH ALL THAT?

I GOT A FEW CALLS FROM REPORTERS WANT-ING TO TALK TO HIM. NO ONE EVER SHOWED UP AT MY HOUSE, THOUGH.

SABRINA'S FAMILY WERE THE ONES GETTING BOM-BARDED. I'VE BEEN IN TOUCH WITH HER SISTER, SANDRA. THEY JUST PUT A STATEMENT ON THE INTERNET AND TRIED TO IGNORE ALL THE INSANITY.

THEN THAT BIG SHOOTING HAPPENED IN BUFFALO LIKE THREE DAYS LATER, SO THE NEWS SHIFTED TO THAT.

I SAW A PICTURE OF THE GUY, THAT YANCEY GUY. IT'S HARD TO BELIEVE HE COULD DO SOMETHING LIKE THAT. I MEAN PHYSICALLY.

WELL, HE DID.

YEA, I KNOW. IT'S JUST WEIRD. THEY SAID HE DIDN'T EVEN OWN A CAR.

LIKE I SAID, I CAN'T READ MUCH ABOUT IT. THE WHOLE THING IS A NIGHTMARE.

THIS JOB USED TO STRESS ME OUT, BUT NOW IT'S A RELIEF TO GET OUT OF MY HOUSE AND COME HERE.

DO YOU THINK YOU MIGHT TAKE THAT JOB IN THE OFFICE OF SPECIAL INVESTIGATIONS?

WHAT? YOU KNEW ABOUT THAT?

YEA. I MEAN, I HEARD ABOUT THE POSITION, AND THAT YOU WERE BEING CONSIDERED, BUT I THOUGHT YOU WERE MOVING TO FLORIDA.

WELL, THAT WAS THE PLAN, BUT I TALKED TO MY EX RECENTLY AND NOW I'M NOT SO SURE.

WHAT HAPPENED?

I JUST GOT HER TO ADMIT THAT SHE REALLY DIDN'T WANT ME MOVING THERE. SHE'S BEEN AVOIDING THE SUBJECT FOR A WHILE.

I WANTED US TO BE A FAMILY AGAIN, BUT IT'S CLEAR SHE DOESN'T WANT THAT ANYMORE.

I'M SORRY TO HEAR THAT.

WELL, WE WERE ACTUALLY TALKING ABOUT THAT JOB IN O.S.I. AND WE BOTH AGREED THAT IT WOULD BE THE BEST THING FOR MY FUTURE.

OH. REALLY?

YEA. I DON'T HAVE A JOB LINED UP IN FLORIDA OR ANYTHING. AND THE PAY BUMP WOULD REALLY HELP ME PROVIDE FOR MY DAUGHTER.

SO THAT'S THE PLAN RIGHT NOW. WE'LL SEE WHAT HAPPENS.

YEA.

I HOPE THIS DOESN'T BOTHER YOU, BUT I'VE BEEN TALKING TO SERGEANT SMITH ABOUT THE POSITION AS WELL.

I REALLY DIDN'T THINK I WAS STEPPING ON YOUR TOES. I DIDN'T GET THE IMPRESSION YOU WERE EVEN PURSUING IT.

AND LOOK, I THINK YOU'RE A BETTER CANDIDATE FOR THE JOB ANYWAY.

YEA, WELL, WHATEVER. DON'T WORRY ABOUT IT.

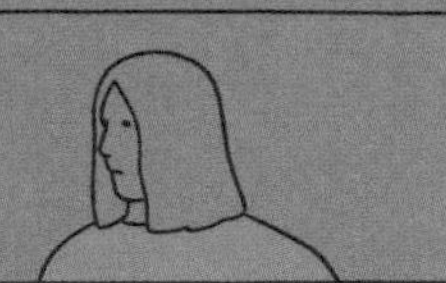
THERE'S BEEN AN OVERWHELMINGLY POSITIVE RESPONSE TO LAST NIGHT'S SHOW IN THE E-MAIL I HAVE HERE. YOUR SUPPORT IS TRULY APPRECIATED.

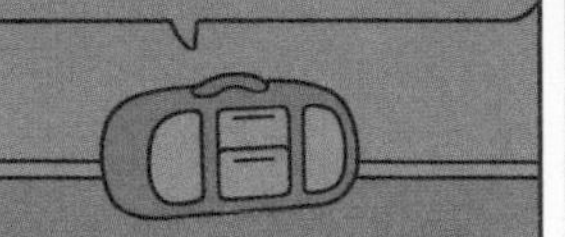
IT'S WONDERFUL TO SEE THE LINES OF COMMUNICATION OPENING. I CAN FEEL THIS THING BEGINNING TO COALESCE. NO LONGER ARE WE SHUT UP IN OUR HOMES, ISOLATED AND FRIGHTENED.

TAKE ONE LONELY PERSON CLACKING AWAY AT A KEYBOARD: POWERLESS. PUT THEM ALL TOGETHER, AND YOU HAVE A FORCE TO BE RECKONED WITH THAT CAN MOVE MOUNTAINS.

LET'S PROVE THAT WE CAN RALLY AROUND A COMMON GOAL. LET'S FOSTER AN INCLUSIVE COMMUNITY OF CONCERNED CITIZENS AND SKEPTICAL WATCHDOGS.

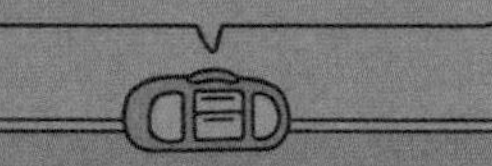
I DON'T THINK I HAVE SOME DIVINE RIGHT TO BE SPOKESPERSON. I FLOAT SOME IDEAS, COMMENT ON THE WORLD AS I SEE IT, AND IT SEEMS TO RESONATE WITH SOME OF YOU. OUR NUMBERS GO UP WITH EACH BROADCAST.

AM I A TYPICAL AMERICAN? MORE TO THE POINT-AM I A TYPICAL HUMAN BEING? I WOULD HOPE SO. I HAVE AN UNCONDITIONAL LOVE FOR MY WIFE AND GIRLS, AN ALMOST PRIMAL NEED TO PROTECT THEM.

I HOLD DOORS OPEN FOR PEOPLE AND TIP TWENTY PERCENT. I WOULD NEVER BE RUDE OR CONDESCEND TO ANYONE IN THE SERVICE INDUSTRY TRYING TO SUPPORT A FAMILY ON MINIMUM WAGE.

I DON'T LIKE THESE BULLIES RUNNING AROUND TREATING DECENT PEOPLE LIKE DISPENSABLE COGS. THESE GUYS TAKE A WAITER OR A SCHOOLTEACHER AND STAND ON THEIR NECKS UNTIL THEY'RE NEARLY SUFFOCATED.

AND AT THE END OF A TWELVE HOUR WORK DAY, WHEN OUR PAYCHECKS ARE SUFFICIENTLY ROBBED AND OUR GOVERNMENT PROGRAMS ARE PRACTICALLY USELESS AND OUR INFRASTRUCTURE IS CRUMBLING, THEY'LL STILL PUT US ON A PLANE AND FLY IT INTO A BUILDING. THEY WILL STILL SEND THE EXECUTIONER INTO AN ELEMENTARY SCHOOL TO MURDER OUR CHILDREN. THEY WILL STILL POISON OUR FOOD AND SPIKE OUR MEDICINE. AND THEY WILL STILL SEND YOU TO JAIL FOR NOT PAYING FOR THE PRIVILEGE.

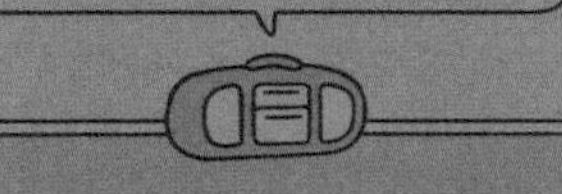
I DON'T LIKE FEELING RESTRAINED. IT'S THIS FEELING LIKE YOU WANT TO RUN AND PLAY, INNOCENT AND CAREFREE, AND THIS FATHER FIGURE IS HOLDING YOU BACK. I DON'T WANT ANY PART OF IT.

I'M SERIOUS. I WANT OUT.

WE WON'T STAND FOR IT MUCH LONGER.

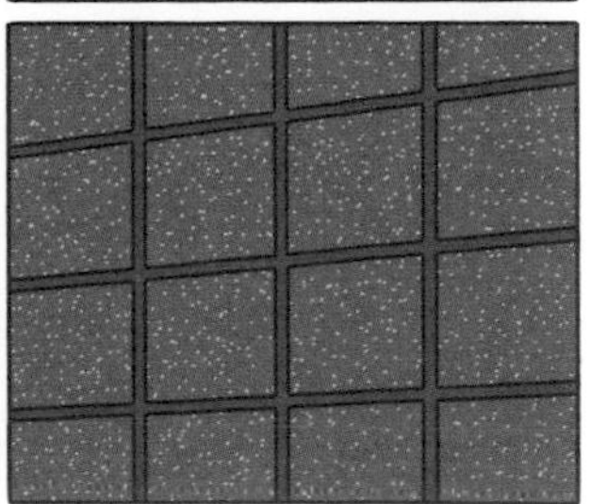

HEY! WANNA GET SOME BREAKFAST?
WHAT LOOKS GOOD?
MM
THANK YOU. I REALLY APPRECIATE IT.

HOW HAVE YOU BEEN FEELING LATELY?
YEA...

ANGRY.

MM

WELL, THAT'S HEALTHY AT LEAST.

DON'T WANT TO BE ALL PENT UP, YOU KNOW? IT MEANS YOU'RE PROCESSING EVERYTHING, I GUESS.

I AM SO ANGRY AT EVERYBODY.

WHO?

EVERYONE. MYSELF.

WELL, THE ONLY PERSON TRULY RESPONSIBLE IS DEAD, SO AT LEAST --

THERE'S PLENTY MORE WHERE HE CAME FROM.

YEA, BUT YOU DON'T WANT TO LASH OUT AT PEOPLE IN GENERAL.

I DIDN'T ASK FOR THIS SITUATION, MAN. SHE DIDN'T DO ANYTHING TO DESERVE THIS SHIT.

NO, OF COURSE NOT.

A LOT OF PEOPLE ARE ABLE TO TURN THEIR GRIEF INTO SOMETHING POSITIVE. MAYBE YOU'RE DESTINED FOR SOME KIND OF JOB IN LAW ENFORCEMENT.

I DON'T KNOW ABOUT THAT.

WELL, WHAT ABOUT CHARITY WORK? HELPING OTHER PEOPLE MIGHT MAKE YOU FEEL BETTER. THERE ARE SOME PLACES TO VOLUNTEER RIGHT HERE IN TOWN.

AND NO, I'M NOT TRYING TO GET YOU OUT OF THE HOUSE.

HEH.

SERIOUSLY, I DON'T THINK SO MUCH ISOLATION IS GOOD FOR YOU RIGHT NOW. WE COULD EVEN HANG OUT WITH MY FRIENDS FROM WORK SOME TIME.

HM.

BLACK FRIDAY DEALS!

WHAT DO YOU DO AT YOUR JOB?

ME? I'M WHAT'S CALLED A BOUNDARY TECHNICIAN.

WHAT'S THAT?

WE HAVE OUR NETWORKS, RIGHT? YOU KNOW, SENSITIVE INFORMATION IS BEING EXCHANGED ELECTRONICALLY ACROSS THE GLOBE. I LOOK FOR WEAKNESSES IN THE SYSTEM, UPDATE FIREWALLS, INVESTIGATE POSSIBLE SECURITY BREACHES.

THAT'S IT?

I WISH I HAD AN EXCITING STORY FOR YOU, BUT I WORK IN A CUBICLE. MINE IS A DESK JOB, TRULY.

EVER FLOWN ANY DRONES?

ME? NO, NOTHING LIKE THAT.

YOU KNOW, IT'S CALLED THE DEPARTMENT OF DEFENSE, NOT THE DE-PARTMENT OF OFFENSE. MOST OF OUR EFFORTS ARE DEVOTED TO SECUR-ITY AND SURVEILLANCE.

WE ALL MAKE FUN OF THOSE COMMERCIALS THAT MAKE THE AIR FORCE LOOK LIKE AN ACTION MOVIE.

--THE VOTE IS SCHED-ULED TO GO BEFORE CONGRESS THIS EVENING.

YEP.

--SIGNIFICANT CUTS TO SOCIAL PROGRAMS AND AN INCREASE IN--

DO YOU WANT TO KNOW WHY THIS RESTAURANT IS EMPTY?

YEA.

THIS USED TO BE A CLAS-SIC, GREASY SPOON, ALL-AMERICAN KIND OF DINER.

UNTIL LAST YEAR, WHEN THE HEALTH INSPECTOR CAME IN AND NEARLY SHUT THE PLACE DOWN. THEY HAD TO REPLACE THEIR KITCHEN EQUIPMENT, CLEAN ALL THE GREASE OFF THE WALLS, REPLACE THE VENTILATION.

NOW, FOR SOME REASON, THE FOOD JUST DOESN'T TASTE AS GOOD. PEOPLE REALLY WANTED IT TO STAY THE SAME, BUT THEY COULDN'T RECRE-ATE THE TASTE.

MY FRIEND CONNOR CALLED IT A CASUALTY OF PROGRESS. HEH...

I ONLY COME BACK BE-CAUSE JACKIE AND I USED TO EAT HERE WITH CICI ALL THE TIME.

I SHOULD TAKE PIC-TURES OF THIS PLACE BEFORE IT SHUTS DOWN. WOULD THAT BE WEIRD?

I DON'T THINK SO.

AD HERE
U.S. | World | Politics | Opinion |
TOP STORIES
NEWS + BUZZ
DAHLMAN
US AIR FORCE
Breaking News
Chicago Execution Video Surfaces on the Net
Man Sentenced for Filming Crash
Advertisement (0:30)
Chicago Execution...
Published November 7, 2017
Emotional blow for a family still reeling from the brutal death of their

HEY.

OH. HEY, CALVIN.

WHAT'S UP?

NOTHING.

DO YOU WANT TO HAVE A CIGARETTE?

UH, YEA SURE. I CAN DO THAT.

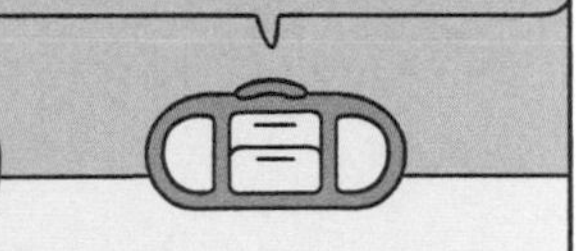
WHAT I'M TALKING ABOUT IS THE ORDER OF CHOSEN MEN WHO INHERIT POW-ER. FROM PHARAOHS AND KINGS TO BANKERS AND EXECUTIVES.

THEIR PATH IS PAVED FOR THEM, AND LIFE IS BUT A CHILD'S LAVISH PLAY PEN.

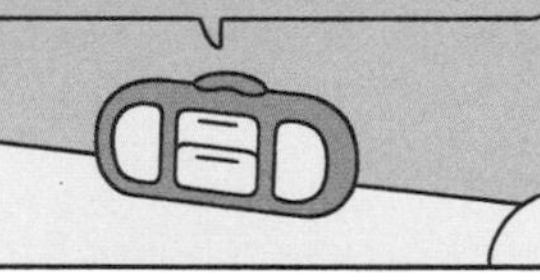
IT USED TO BE THAT THE PEASANTS WOULD TOIL IN MEANINGLESS SERVITUDE, UNABLE TO SEE THE BIG PICTURE, WITHOUT A CHANCE TO BREAK THE CYCLE.

NOW WE HAVE COMPUTERS TO HELP US DO OUR RE-SEARCH. SUDDENLY, THE RHYTHMS AND PATTERNS OF OPPRESSION AND DE-CEIT SINCE TIME IM-MEMORIAL COME INTO STARTLING FOCUS.

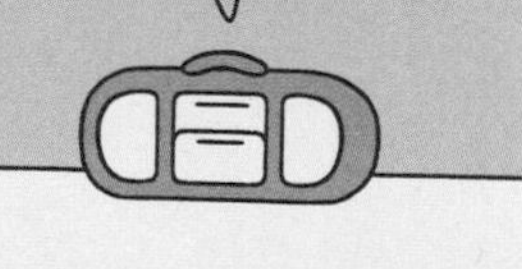
I WANT TO GET TO SOME FASCINATING MATERIAL ABOUT PRINCE BERNHARD THAT WAS SENT IN BY A LISTENER.

BUT FIRST, THERE'S SOMETHING ELSE I NEED TO TALK ABOUT.

HERE WE HAVE ANOTHER PIECE OF THE FEAR MONGERING CAMPAIGN, WHICH SEEMS TO KNOW NO END OR LIMITS OF DEPRAVITY.

IT MAKES PERFECT SENSE, ACTUALLY. AN INNOCENT PERSON WALKS DOWN A STREET IN AMERICA, NOW THEIR EXECUTION IS BEING DOWNLOADED ABOUT FIVE MILLION TIMES PER HOUR.

THIS TAPS INTO THE DEEPEST FEARS THAT MAN CAN CONJURE, BUT ALSO OUR MORBID DESIRE TO SEE THESE THINGS.

BE HONEST, HOW MANY OF YOU ARE AT YOUR COMPUTER RIGHT NOW, TRYING TO FIND THIS VIDEO? I HAVE TO GIVE THEM CREDIT, THEY KNOW HOW TO CAPTIVATE AN AUDIENCE.

NOW, YOU'RE ALL ASKING ME WHAT THIS MEANS. WHAT IS REALLY GOING ON HERE? IT'S JUST TOO EARLY TO TELL, BUT IT HAS ALL THE HALLMARKS OF THE STAGED TRAGEDIES THAT HAVE BECOME SO ROUTINE, EACH MORE HORRIFIC THAN THE LAST. WE ARE NOW THOROUGHLY DESENSITIZED. IT'S AS IF THESE GUYS ARE TRYING TO OUTDO EACH OTHER FOR OUR ATTENTION.

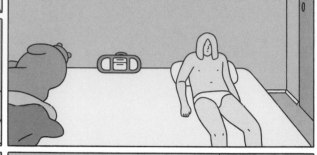

THE SANITIZED INFORMATION IS AVAILABLE FROM WHEN THIS STORY BROKE TWO MONTHS AGO. I ENCOURAGE ALL OF YOU AMATEUR SLEUTHS OUT THERE TO READ THROUGH IT CLOSELY, LOOKING FOR THE DISCREPANCIES, INACCURACIES, DISTORTIONS, AND OUTRIGHT LIES THAT SEEM SO EASY TO SPOT IF YOU'VE TRAINED YOUR CYNICAL EYE.

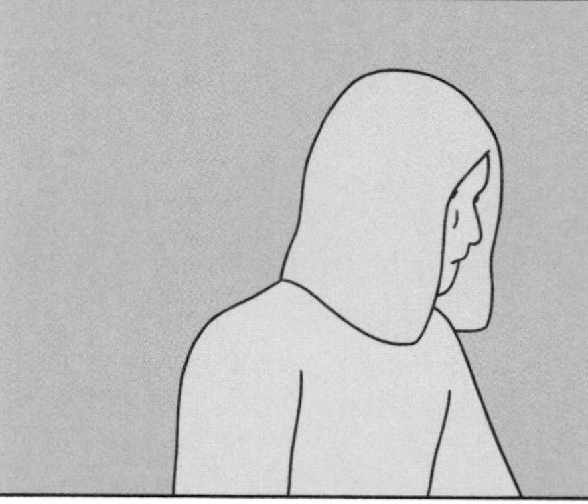

AS A RULE, I WOULD SAY THAT ANY REPORTING THAT CAN BE TRACED BACK TO A HANDFUL OF PARENT CORPORATIONS CAN BE IMMEDIATELY DISMISSED AS FICTION.

I HAVEN'T GOTTEN A CHANCE TO STUDY THE VIDEO TOO CLOSELY. I'LL DO MY PART, AND WE CAN GET TO THE BOTTOM OF THIS THING. WHAT ARE THEY TRYING TO SAY WITH THIS ONE? DON'T LEAVE YOUR HOUSE? DON'T TRUST YOUR NEIGHBOR? SUBMIT YOURSELF TO A MARTIAL LAW POLICE STATE?

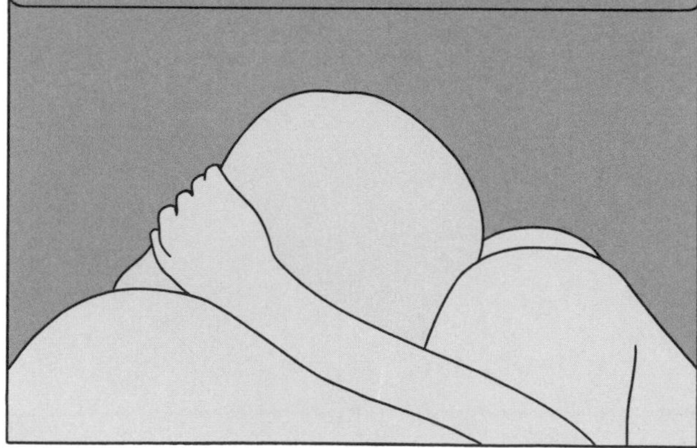

IF YOU'RE WILLING TO BELIEVE THE OFFICIAL STORY, THAT AN ARCHETYPAL LONER WITH NO RESOURCES ABDUCTED AND SLAUGHTERED A TOTAL STRANGER IN HIS SMALL APARTMENT FOR NO REASON, BY ALL MEANS, PULL THAT WOOL A LITTLE BIT TIGHTER. THERE IS SOMETHING MORE COMPLICATED AT WORK, YOU CAN BE SURE OF THAT.

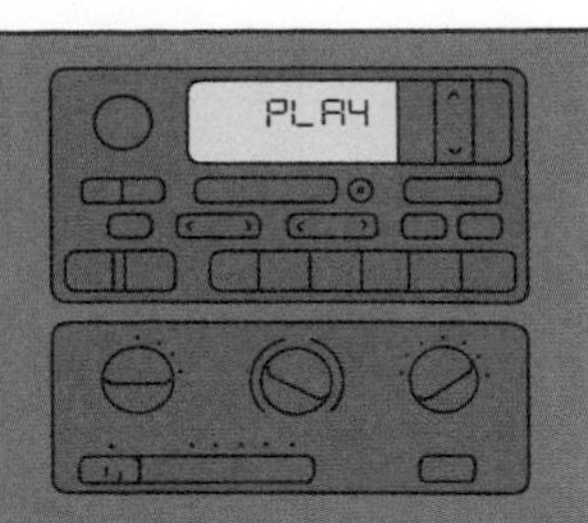

PLAY

WHAT THE FUCK IS THIS?

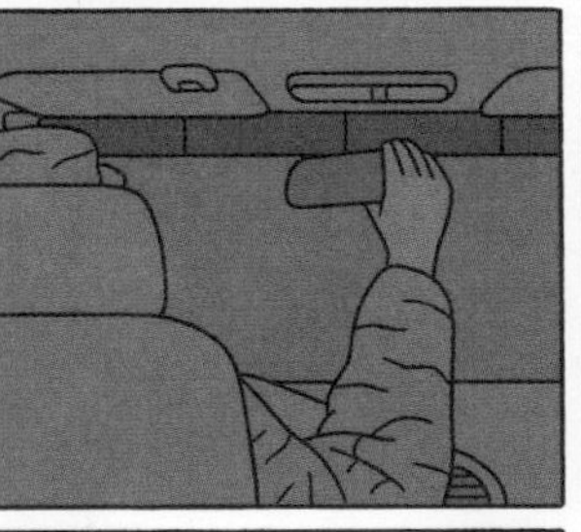

KTTV

MR. WROBEL, SIR! CAN WE TALK TO YOU FOR A MOMENT?

WHAT IS THIS?

IS MR. TEDDY KING STILL WITH YOU? WE WERE HOPING TO SPEAK TO HIM.

WHAT'S GOING ON?

THE NEW DEVELOPMENT WITH THE VIDEO LEAK-ING ON THE INTERNET.

WHAT?

HOW HAS MR. KING BEEN HOLDING UP?

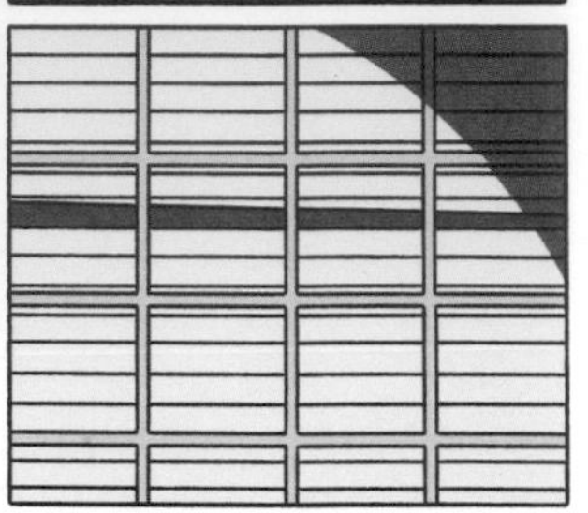

I, UH...

DO YOU HAVE ANYTHING TO SAY ABOUT THE SITUATION?

JESUS. NO. I, UM...

IF YOU COULD JUST GIVE US A COMMENT, CALVIN.

I REALLY DON'T HAVE ANYTHING TO SAY.

WELL, IF YOU COULD MAYBE TALK TO MR. KING AND SEE IF HE WOULD BE WILLING TO-

NO. I HAVE TO GO INSIDE.

WHAT DO YOU THINK ABOUT THE-

LOOK. I ASKED YOU NICELY. PLEASE RE-SPECT OUR PRIVACY. I DON'T EVEN KNOW WHY YOU'RE ASKING ME ABOUT THIS. I DIDN'T EVEN KNOW SANDRA.

PLEASE, I DON'T WANT YOU GUYS OUT HERE. YOU ARE GONNA UPSET HIM.
CAN I GIVE YOU MY CARD?
GET OFF MY PROPERTY. I'M SERIOUS!
JUST GO! I HAVE TO GO INSIDE.
TEDDY?
HELLO?
TEDDY. CAN I TALK TO YOU?
PLEASE OPEN THE DOOR!
HELLO?
COME ON, MAN. ARE YOU ALL RIGHT?

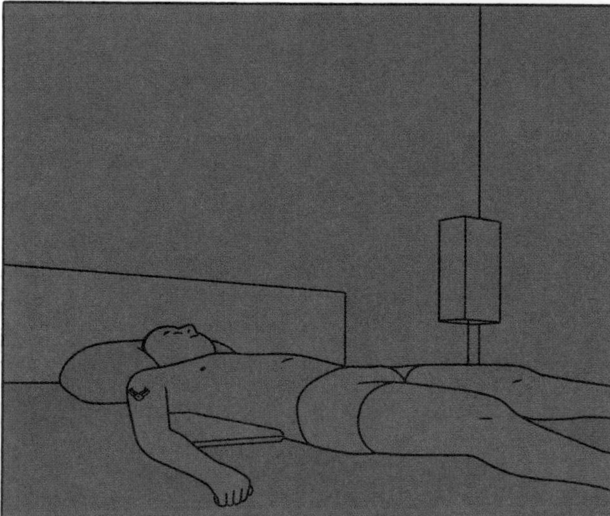

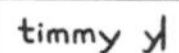

Story by Zach David Olsen
Follow: @zdolsen

Skip Ahead:
Part 1: Troubled Beginnings
Part 2: A Thrill of Hope
Part 3: Undoing
Part 4: The Victim
Part 5: Who is to Blame?
Part 6: What Have We Learned?

Published 11·7·2017
Chicago Execution-
A Family Reacts
·Updated 52 minutes ago

Emotions Boil for Sister
of Slain Chicagoan

>> This is madness!
>> This has to stop!

>> Get away from me!

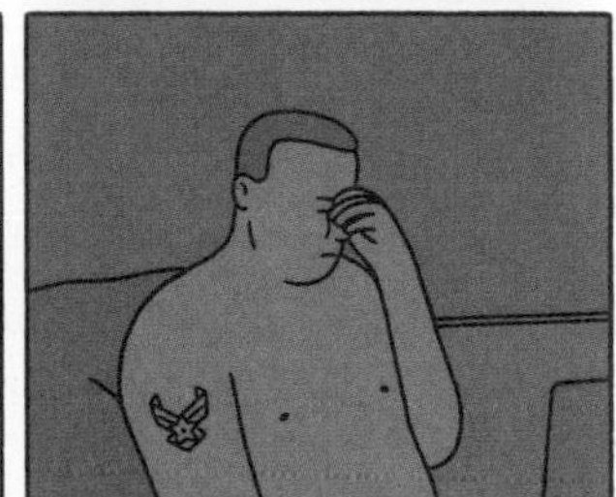

timmy yancey video
timmy yancey video
timmy yancey video leak
timmy yancey video download
timmy yancey video full
timmy yancey video stream
timmy yancey video zip

AD:
DOWNLOAD NOW!
AD:
Tired of waiting?
UPGRADE!

YOUR DOWNLOAD
IS COMPLETE!
WOOHOO!!
CLICK
to open

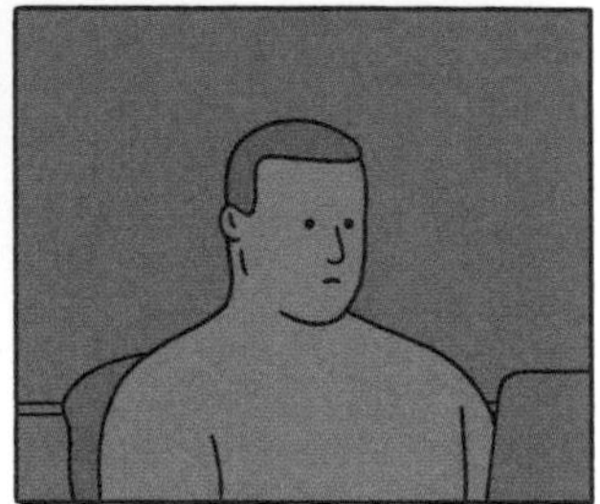

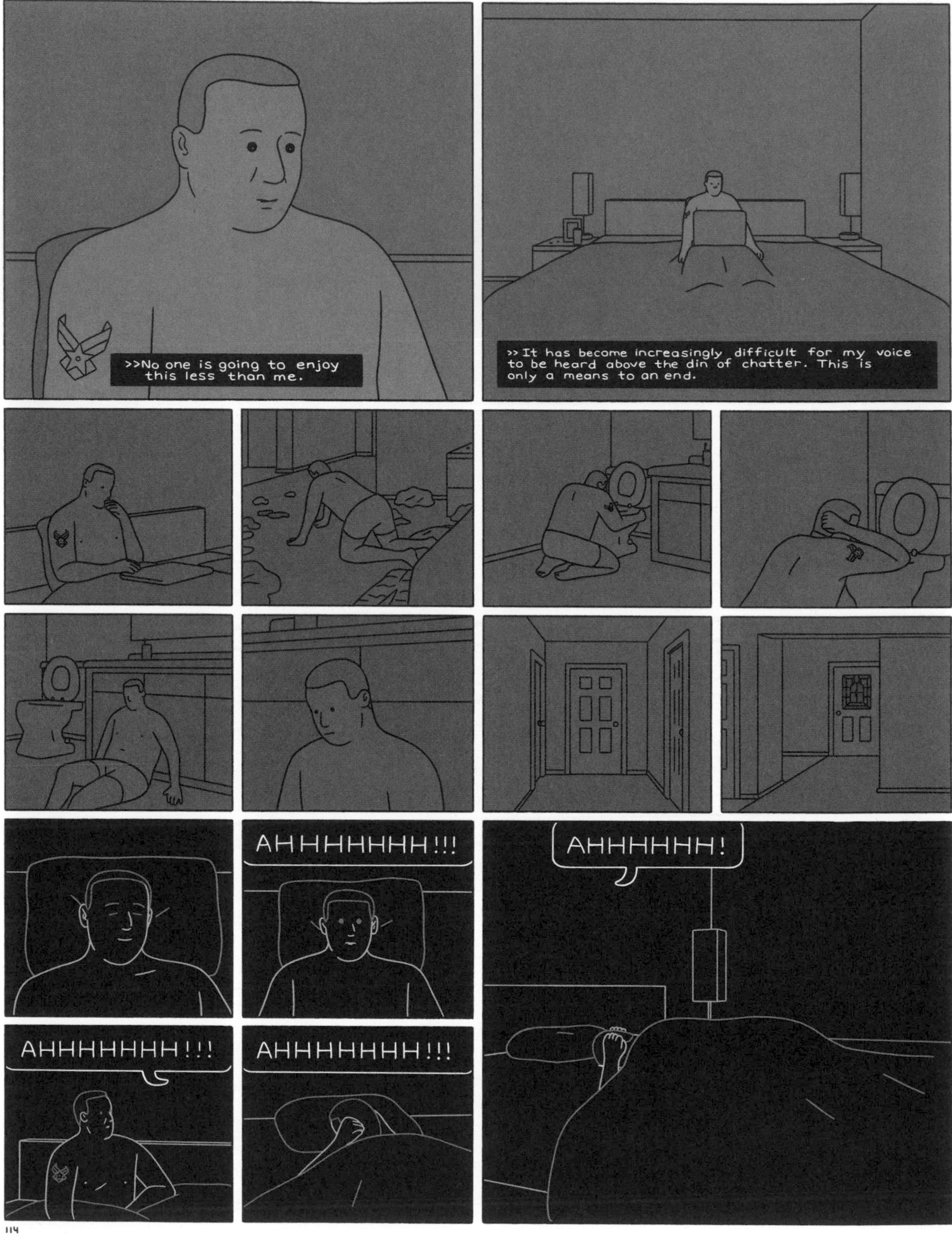
>>No one is going to enjoy this less than me.
>>It has become increasingly difficult for my voice to be heard above the din of chatter. This is only a means to an end.
AHHHHHHH!!!
AHHHHHH!
AHHHHHHH!!!
AHHHHHHH!!!

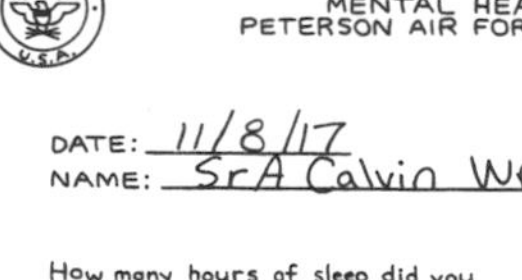

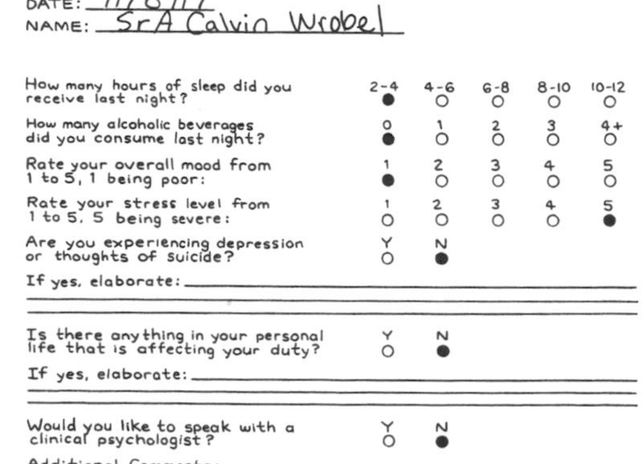

DOD MEDICAL EVALUATION REVIEW BOARD
MENTAL HEALTH SURVEY
PETERSON AIR FORCE BASE COLORADO

DATE: 11/8/17
NAME: SrA Calvin Wrobel

How many hours of sleep did you receive last night?	2-4 ●	4-6 ○	6-8 ○	8-10 ○	10-12 ○
How many alcoholic beverages did you consume last night?	0 ●	1 ○	2 ○	3 ○	4+ ○
Rate your overall mood from 1 to 5, 1 being poor:	1 ●	2 ○	3 ○	4 ○	5 ○
Rate your stress level from 1 to 5, 5 being severe:	1 ○	2 ○	3 ○	4 ○	5 ●
Are you experiencing depression or thoughts of suicide?	Y ○	N ●			

If yes, elaborate: ______

Is there anything in your personal life that is affecting your duty?	Y ○	N ●

If yes, elaborate: ______

Would you like to speak with a clinical psychologist?	Y ○	N ●

Additional Comments: ______

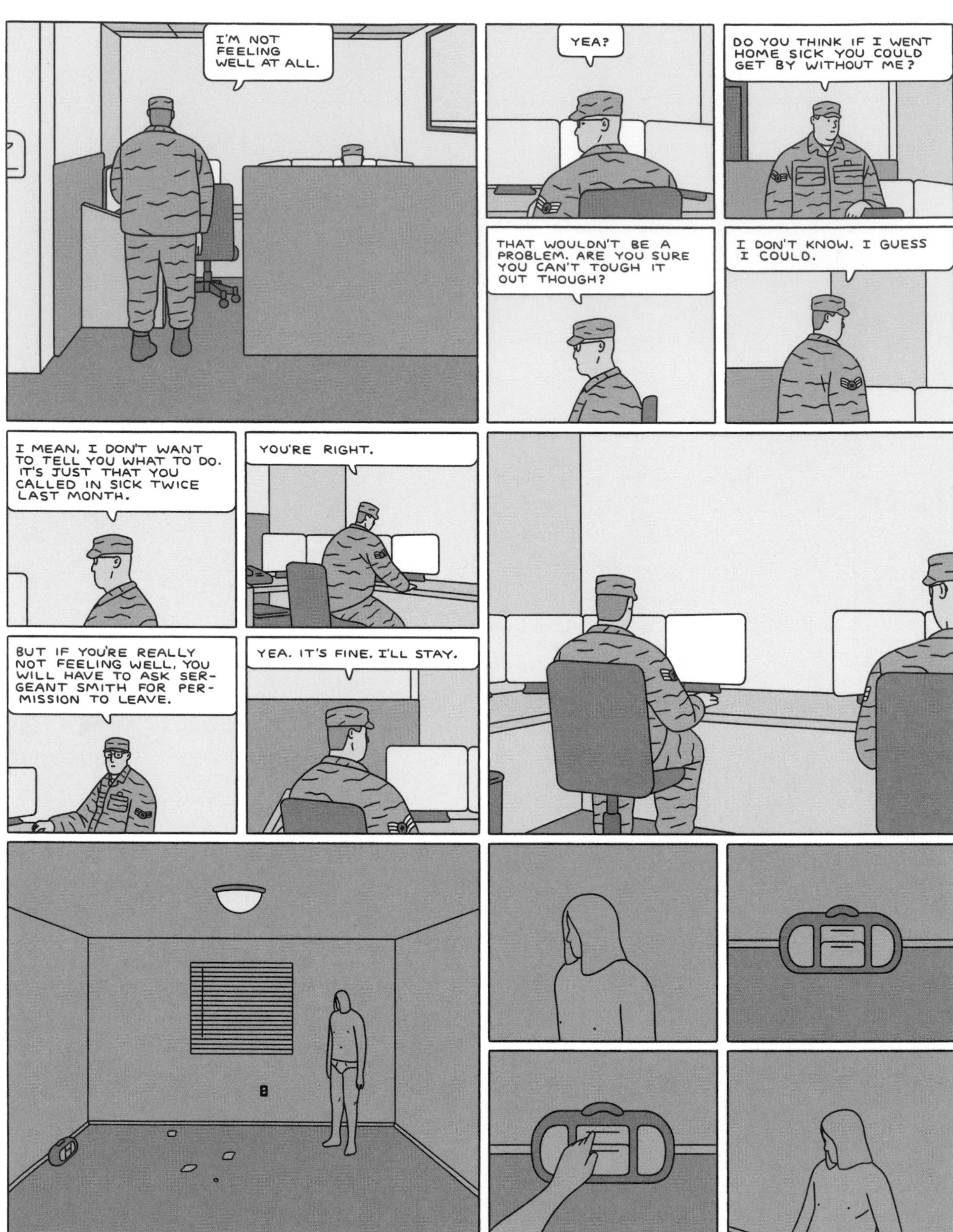
I'M NOT FEELING WELL AT ALL.
YEA?
DO YOU THINK IF I WENT HOME SICK YOU COULD GET BY WITHOUT ME?
THAT WOULDN'T BE A PROBLEM. ARE YOU SURE YOU CAN'T TOUGH IT OUT THOUGH?
I DON'T KNOW. I GUESS I COULD.
I MEAN, I DON'T WANT TO TELL YOU WHAT TO DO. IT'S JUST THAT YOU CALLED IN SICK TWICE LAST MONTH.
YOU'RE RIGHT.
BUT IF YOU'RE REALLY NOT FEELING WELL, YOU WILL HAVE TO ASK SER-GEANT SMITH FOR PER-MISSION TO LEAVE.
YEA. IT'S FINE. I'LL STAY.

WELL, HERE WE ARE. WELCOME TO THE SHOW EVERYBODY.

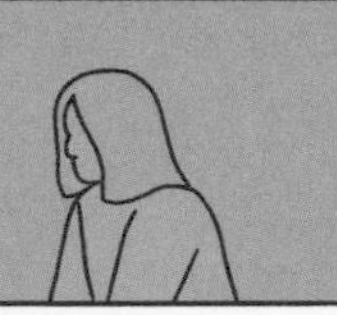

WE'VE HAD SOME BEAUTIFUL WEATHER LATELY. CRISP AND REFRESHING. HOPE YOU'RE ALL ENJOYING IT AS MUCH AS I AM.

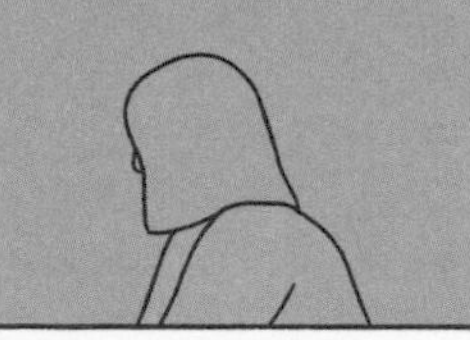

LET'S NOT WASTE ANY TIME. THE VIDEO FROM CHICAGO IS ON EVERYONE'S MIND.

THE MAINSTREAM MEDIA ARE CALLING IT THE MOST SADISTIC ACT OF RANDOM VIOLENCE WE'VE SEEN DOMESTICALLY IN DECADES. THE INTERNET IS RIFE WITH RUMORS AND SPECULATION. WE ARE ALL SEARCHING FOR MEANING.

LIKE MANY OF YOU, I RECOILED IN DISGUST. IT IS TRULY A TERRIFYING SIGHT. BUT YOU MUST RESIST YOUR INITIAL REACTION. DON'T LET THEM MANIPULATE YOUR EMOTIONS. TRY TO EXAMINE IT LIKE A FROG IN FORMALDEHYDE.

THERE ARE CERTAIN NAGGING QUESTIONS WE MUST CONSIDER. YANCEY'S WEIGHT WHEN HE DIED WAS REPORTEDLY ONE-HUNDRED-TEN POUNDS. DOES THE MAN IN THE VIDEO APPEAR TO WEIGH ONE-HUNDRED-TEN POUNDS?

WHY DOES HE STOP RECORDING AT ONE POINT, AND APPEAR TO TALK TO SOMEONE OFF-CAMERA? ARE THESE THE RAMBLINGS OF A DISTURBED YOUNG MAN, OR THE FINAL MOMENTS OF TWO PEOPLE HELD HOSTAGE?

I'M ALSO WONDERING WHY HE WOULD HIDE HIS FACE BEHIND A MASK IF HE CRAVED NOTORIETY FOR HIS CRIME. IS IT BECAUSE HE'S NOT THE EXECUTIONER AT ALL?

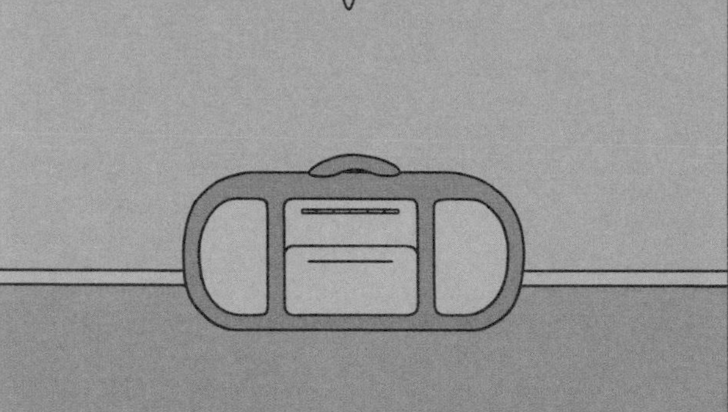

IT'S ALSO WORTH POINTING OUT THAT MANY LINES FROM HIS TIRADE WERE TAKEN FROM HIS OWN PAST WRITINGS ON DIFFERENT ONLINE FORUMS. WHY WOULD HE REUSE THINGS HE'D ALREADY SAID? LEADS ME TO BELIEVE HIS SPEECH WAS DRAFTED BY SOMEONE WHO WANTED TO MAKE IT APPEAR TO BE WRITTEN BY HIM.

I WON'T MINCE WORDS: I DON'T BELIEVE FOR A SECOND THAT SABRINA GALLO WAS KILLED BY TIMMY YANCEY. THE VIDEO JUST LOOKS UNBELIEVABLE. I DON'T BELIEVE SOMETHING LIKE THAT COULD HAPPEN.

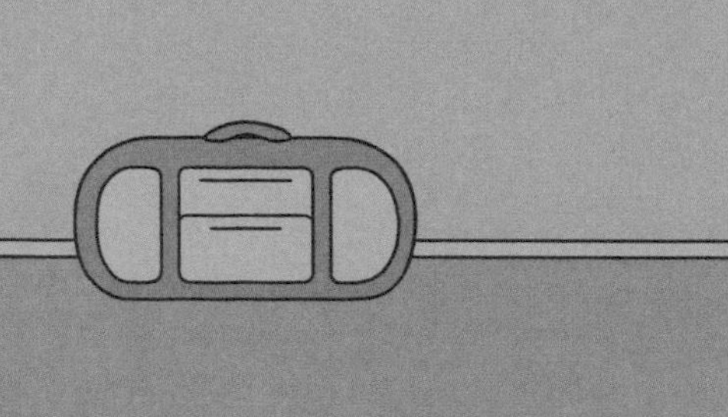

FOR ALL WE KNOW, SHE'S ALIVE IN BONDAGE SOMEWHERE. OR SHE COULD BE AN ACTRESS WEARING PROSTHETICS TO CONCEAL HER IDENTITY. IT'S POSSIBLE SHE NEVER EVEN EXISTED. WE KNOW THE MILITARY HAS ACCESS TO ADVANCED COMPUTER-GENERATED IMAGE TECHNOLOGY THAT THE PUBLIC WON'T BE AWARE OF FOR ANOTHER TEN YEARS.

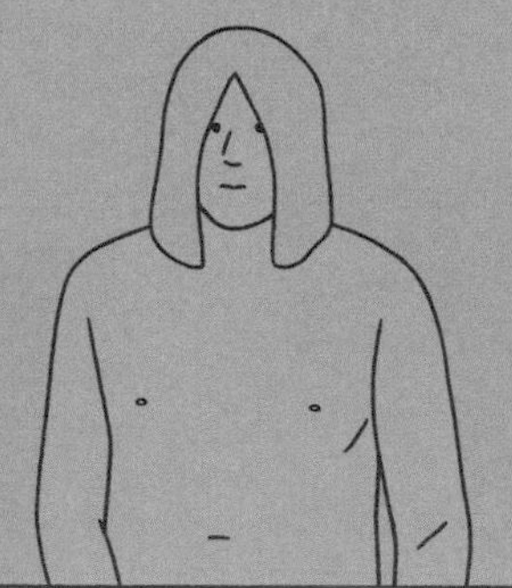

MAYBE FORCES TOO EVIL TO COMPREHEND DID IN FACT MURDER A WOMAN NAMED SABRINA GALLO. I JUST DON'T THINK A MAN NAMED TIMMY YANCEY IS RESPONSIBLE.

WHEN THE HYSTERIA SUBSIDES, THIS VIDEO IS DESTINED TO BE ANOTHER RELIC THAT WE WILL NEVER TRULY UNDERSTAND. A NEW TRAGEDY PRESENTS ITSELF BEFORE WE CAN MAKE SENSE OF THE LAST. WHY DOES THIS KEEP HAPPENING, AND WHO KEEPS DOING THIS TO US? I WISH I COULD STRANGLE THEIR COLLECTIVE NECKS AND BE DONE WITH IT, SO WE COULD BUILD OUR UTOPIA IN PEACE. MAYBE SOME ADVANCED BEING WILL SIFT THROUGH THIS JUNK WHEN WE'RE GONE, AND WONDER HOW SIBLINGS COULD BE SO CRUEL TO EACH OTHER.
NOTHING JUST HAPPENS. EVERY NEWS STORY IS AS STRATEGICALLY MANUFACTURED AS THE ADS WEDGED BETWEEN THEM. THERE'S A STORY ABOUT HOUSING PRICES. THERE'S A COMMERCIAL OFFERING CASH FOR GOLD. THERE'S A STORY ABOUT A MASS SHOOTING. THERE'S A COMMERCIAL FOR ANTIDEPRESSANTS. WHEN YOU'RE WILLING TO ACKNOWLEDGE THESE PATTERNS, YOU MIGHT NEVER SLEEP SOUNDLY AGAIN.
THE FEAR OF THE UNKNOWN, THAT DEATH COULD STRIKE IN THE SAFEST PLACE, IS ESSENTIAL TO THE PARANOIA CAMPAIGN. THINK ABOUT IT. IN THE PAST FEW YEARS WE'VE SEEN ATTACKS IN A GRADE SCHOOL, A MOVIE THEATER, A CHURCH, A HOSPITAL, AND NEARLY EVERYWHERE IN BETWEEN. DOESN'T THIS TIMMY YANCEY THING SEEM LIKE PART OF AN ESCALATING CONTINUUM?
GIVEN THE GROSS ATROCITIES OF THE SHADOW GOVERNMENT THAT ARE REVEALED AFTER THE FACT — SECRET WARS, ILLEGAL SURVEILLANCE, MIND CONTROL EXPERIMENTS AND THE LIKE — WOULD YOU PUT IT PAST THEM TO KILL ONE OR TWO INNOCENT CIVILIANS IF IT FURTHERED THEIR PLANS?
WHO ARE THESE AGENCIES BUT A COLLECTION OF EMPLOYEES, UNDER CONTRACT, CONCERNED ONLY WITH THEIR CAREERS AND REPUTATIONS? IF A MORAL OBJECTION MEANT LOSING YOUR JOB, YOUR HOME, EVEN YOUR LIFE - COULD YOU BLAME ANY OF THEM FOR THEIR OBEDIENCE? WOULD YOU ACT ANY DIFFERENT?

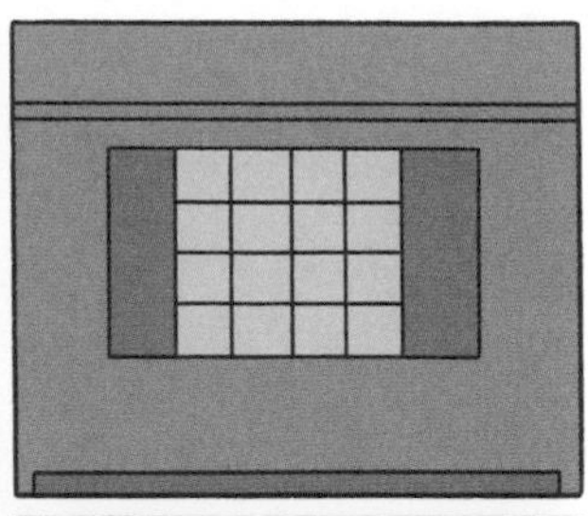

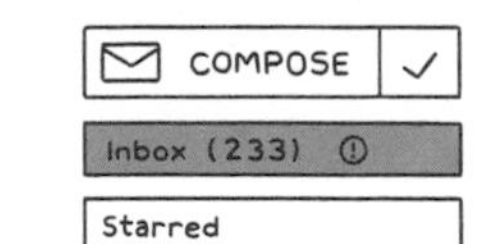

calvin wrobel|

calvin wrobel fake
calvin wrobel actor
calvin wrobel exposed
calvin wrobel teddy king
calvin wrobel interview
calvin wrobel facebook
calvin wrobel air force
calvin wrobel timmy
calvin wrobel youtube

https://www.irontruth.blogs...

IRON TRUTH REPORT

You Can't Stop The People!

Chicago Execution Lies Unfurl - Actor Flubs Line

The hoax almost worked.

Unfortunately for the conspirators, you can't fool us in the digital age. A video appeared yesterday of a young woman being murdered by a man in a mask in Chicago.

The woman's live-in boyfriend has yet to surface, and appears to have fled Illinois to hide out with a friend, who is in the AIR FORCE no less.

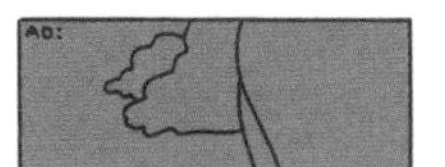

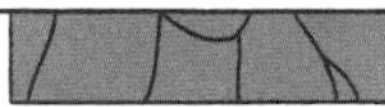

This friend is Calvin Wrobel, who was caught by a news crew outside his home last night. When asked about Sabrina Gallo's death, Wrobel was irritated and hostile.

Watch:

EXPOSED! Conspirator Can't Keep His Lines Straight

...WHAT DID HE SAY??

This man is obviously a phony. The ruse might have worked if he didn't get the victim's NAME wrong. Nice try. Sandra is the victim's sister, or so they would like you to believe. More on that later.

I wonder who he is covering for. How much money do you think this fake im - poster actor was paid to say these lines?

Submit

Total 77 comments

Anonymous

Someone should kill you "Calvin Wrobel."

NOV 8 2017 7:02 PM REPLY

JP

Agreed.

Rodney

Fraud! Your day is coming. We know your lies and will smoke you out where you live.

NOV 8 2017 9:11 REPLY

Sammy

I will not bow to my master. I will not cower in fear. I will not be manipulated.

Mark C.

I'm too smart to be fooled by this hoax. Buncha bullshit. Stay vigilant. >:-(

NOV 8 2017 10:59 REPLY

Anonymous

Outstanding work as always Bill! Thanks for all your hard work bro :)

NOV 8 2017 11:00 REPLY

Ronald

This is what it means to be a man. To assert yourself. To stand up and make yourself heard. To be effective. To reject authority in all its forms. To rape and pillage and run wild in the streets. I love this site for telling it like it is! Rock on!

NOV 8 2017 11:31 REPLY

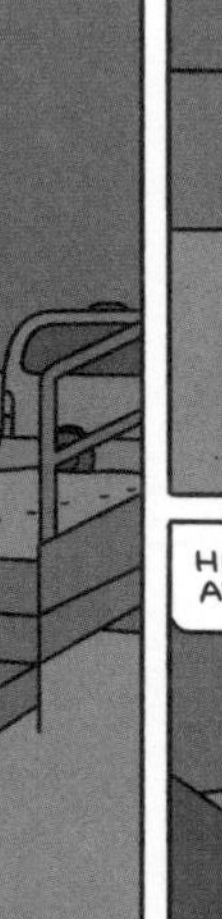

HEY! THE PARK CLOSES AT DUSK.

YEA, I'M SORRY.

DO YOU LIVE IN THIS COMMUNITY?

YES. RIGHT AROUND THE CORNER.

I JUST NEEDED SOME FRESH AIR.

OH. HEY.

WE'RE GONNA NEED YOU TO GO HOME. THIS PARK IS CLOSED.

In the news

After Chicago Execution, 'False Flag' Conspiracy Theories Surface

By Molly O'Connell
November 8 2017

It is now expected that with any highly publicized act of violence comes dissidence and a host of alternative explanations.

A small but vocal minority believe that a global cabal is behind every major tragedy, from the death of a celebrity to the attacks of 9/11 to the murder of an innocent woman.

In the wake of the shooting at Sandy Hook Elementary in which twenty children and six adults were murdered by a single gunman, some parents of the victims were harassed by people who believed they were actors, that their children never even existed, and that they were paid to participate in the cover-up.

This may seem like marginal extremism, but to this day when you type "Sandy Hook" into Google, the first suggested word to add to the search phrase is "fake." The hysteria is spreading, and the reason for this varies wildly, depending on which side you ask.

The killing of Sabrina Gallo is no exception. Within hours, conspiracy websites were already labeling the execution video a hoax, claiming that it was "obviously designed as a fear-mongering distraction."

When a Louisville news program erroneously reported that a third body was found in Timmy Yancey's apartment, then quickly apologized for the mistake, conspiracy theorists used this as proof of deception.

When Calvin Wrobel, a friend of Sabrina Gallo's boyfriend, was stopped by a news crew outside his home last night and referred to the victim by the wrong name, that was used as proof positive of a conspiracy.

The problem with these theories is that they can't be reasoned with. Any fact that doesn't fit the alternative explanation is dismissed as a lie or disinformation. Any avoidance is tacit confirmation. Anyone close to the victim is an actor or being paid to remain silent.

The most troubling detail of the Timmy Yancey story is that he seemed to be a proponent of such radical conspiracy theories. We now know that he listened to the Albert Douglas radio show every day, and frequently wrote on the show's message board, showing support for the ideas espoused by the host.

Timmy Yancey was actually being mourned on one website as an innocent scapegoat that was targeted because of his political beliefs and his online presence in conspiracy theory circles. Concurrently, the same website demonized Sabrina Gallo and her family as somehow being insiders in the plot.

This morning, Sandra Gallo filed a police report, claiming that she received death threats from a man who demanded to know what really happened to her sister. Similar threats are being hurled at Sabrina Gallo's boyfriend, who has not made any public statements.

Despite being staunchly anti-government, Yancey had a curious preoccupation with the military. As a child, he immersed himself in World War II history, and often said he wished he could have been alive to fight. He even wanted to enlist in the army, but his mother discouraged him.

Radio host Albert Douglas served in the army during the Gulf War. It wasn't until after 9/11 and the invasion of Iraq that he became interested in conspiracy theories, and began broadcasting when he was laid off from his job as a postman in 2009.

Since then, he has built a sizable audience by routinely predicting an imminent apocalypse, and claiming that most acts of terrorism are staged by the government as a means to strip the American people of their freedom and push through stricter gun control legislation.

These theories have been given credence by writers and academics such as Harry Drake, a professor at Florida State University who was fired after asking the parents of a child murdered at Sandy Hook to produce a death certificate.

WOULD YOU LIKE ANYTHING ELSE?

NO, THANK YOU.

WE'RE CLOSING IN TWENTY MINUTES. YOU HAVE A GREAT NIGHT.

·WHERE IS SABRINA GALLO?
·ARE THESE PEOPLE EVEN REAL?
????

Is Calvin Wrobel Actor Garry Platz?

One-time sitcom star has found fame once again in latest NWO campaign.

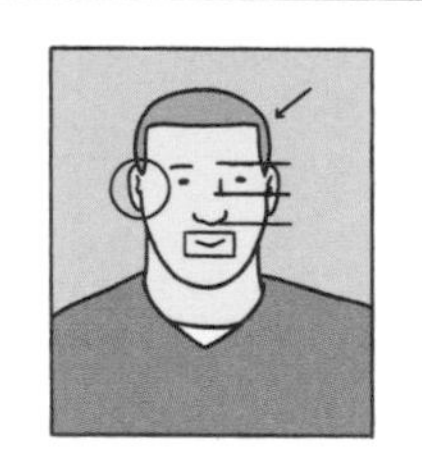

THE ALBERT DOUGLAS RADIO SHOW

DISCUSSION BOARD | ACTIVE TOPICS

SUB-FORUMS:

CHICAGO EXECU... Posts: 6,790 Last: 1 m. ago	9/11 Posts: 847,303 Last: 64 m. ago
CIA Posts: 111,660 Last: 1 day ago	SECRET SOCIET... Posts: 716,318 Last: 2 days ago
MEDIA	WEAPONRY

Timmy Yancey - CIA Mind Controlled Killer -thriller, 11/8/17

Execution Video Analyzed. Fakes and Mistakes. -willis, 11/8/17

Calvin Wrobel - CRISIS ACTOR -strikerman, 11/8/17

Sabrina Gallo Alive! You Won't Believe It! -thislife, 11/8/17

Watch my video! 100% proof! like/comment/subscribe -sunshine, 11/8/17

Gun grab within 72 hours. Arm yourself now! -ComfyChair, 11/8/17

Martial Law expected before Thanksgiving -msProphet, 11/8/17

Sabrina Gallo never existed. "Sister" hired as actress. -Cassman07, 11/8/17

Gallo Family contact info and home addresses. -Questions, 11/8/17

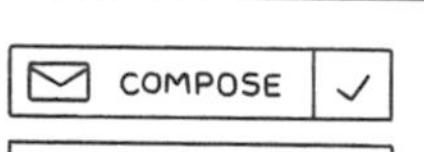

Inbox (313)

Starred

Important

Sent Mail

Drafts

The Truth Will Set You Free

Jason Richmond 2:16 AM
to me

Hi Calvin:

I don't know who you're covering for or what they've done to you, but I must insist that you join us in the good fight.

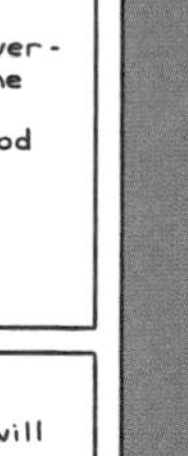

Expose the conspiracy before it's too late. You're going to die anyway, someday. Why not be the greatest American hero who ever lived. You're wielding tremendous power! Can't you see that?

Do you worry about the world your daughter, Cici, will live in? She lives at 2701 Hibiscus Road, Tampa, Florida 33637, right? With your wife, Jackie? It's a dangerous world out there. Please do the right thing. I beg you.

See you soon,
A Warrior for Truth

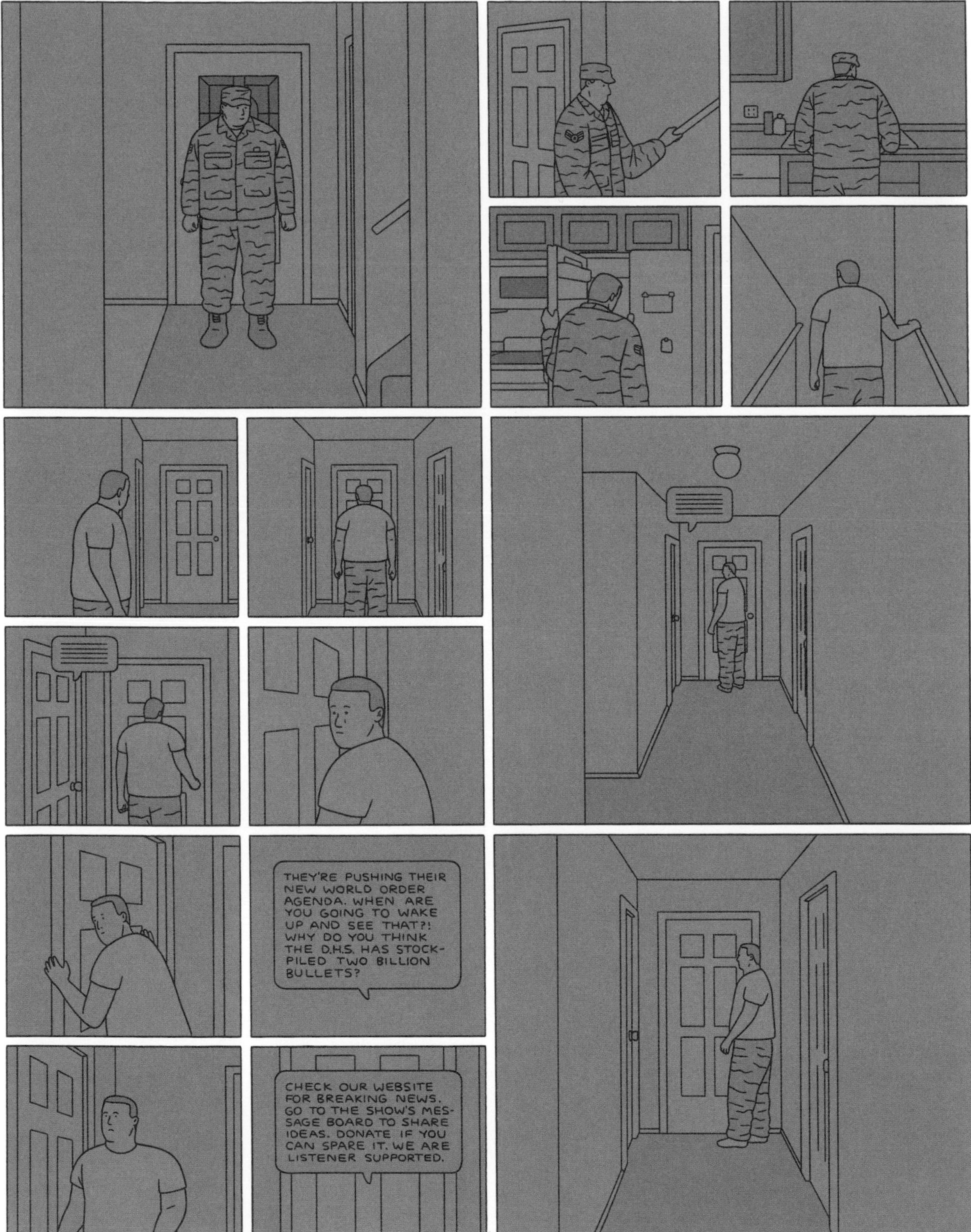
THEY'RE PUSHING THEIR NEW WORLD ORDER AGENDA. WHEN ARE YOU GOING TO WAKE UP AND SEE THAT?! WHY DO YOU THINK THE D.H.S. HAS STOCK-PILED TWO BILLION BULLETS?
CHECK OUR WEBSITE FOR BREAKING NEWS. GO TO THE SHOW'S MES-SAGE BOARD TO SHARE IDEAS. DONATE IF YOU CAN SPARE IT. WE ARE LISTENER SUPPORTED.

SANDRA?
HI.
HOW ARE YOU?
YEA.
DO YOU WANT TO TALK TO TEDDY?
ALL RIGHT. I'LL GO GET HIM.

TEDDY?
I'M COMING IN.
SANDRA'S ON THE PHONE. DO YOU WANT TO TALK TO HER?
I THINK YOU SHOULD.
MM...
COME ON, MAN.
THE PHONE'S ON THE COUNTER. DON'T UNPLUG IT, THOUGH. IT HAS TO CHARGE BEFORE I LEAVE FOR WORK.

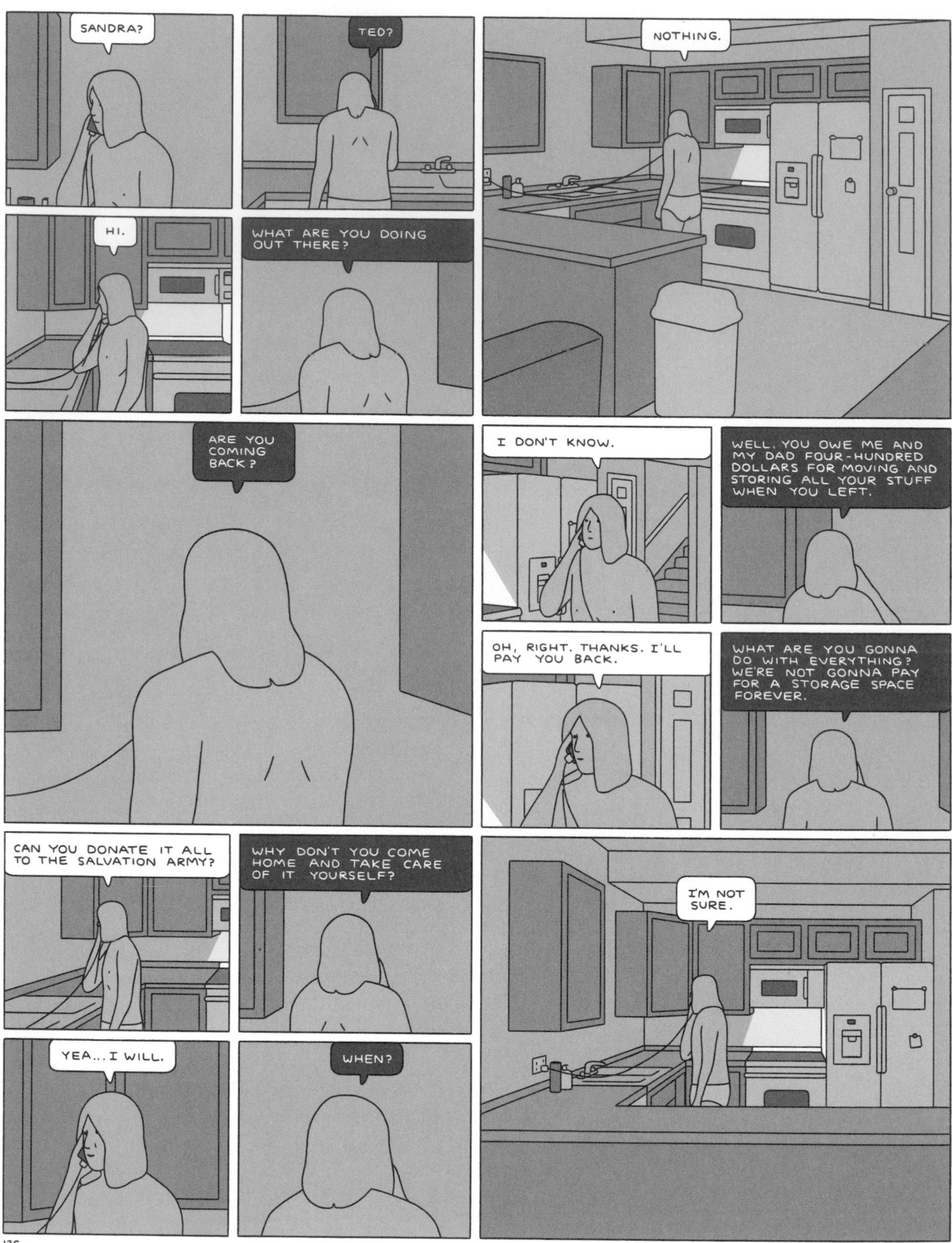
SANDRA?
TED?
NOTHING.
HI.
WHAT ARE YOU DOING OUT THERE?
ARE YOU COMING BACK?
I DON'T KNOW.
WELL, YOU OWE ME AND MY DAD FOUR-HUNDRED DOLLARS FOR MOVING AND STORING ALL YOUR STUFF WHEN YOU LEFT.
OH, RIGHT. THANKS. I'LL PAY YOU BACK.
WHAT ARE YOU GONNA DO WITH EVERYTHING? WE'RE NOT GONNA PAY FOR A STORAGE SPACE FOREVER.
CAN YOU DONATE IT ALL TO THE SALVATION ARMY?
WHY DON'T YOU COME HOME AND TAKE CARE OF IT YOURSELF?
YEA... I WILL.
WHEN?
I'M NOT SURE.

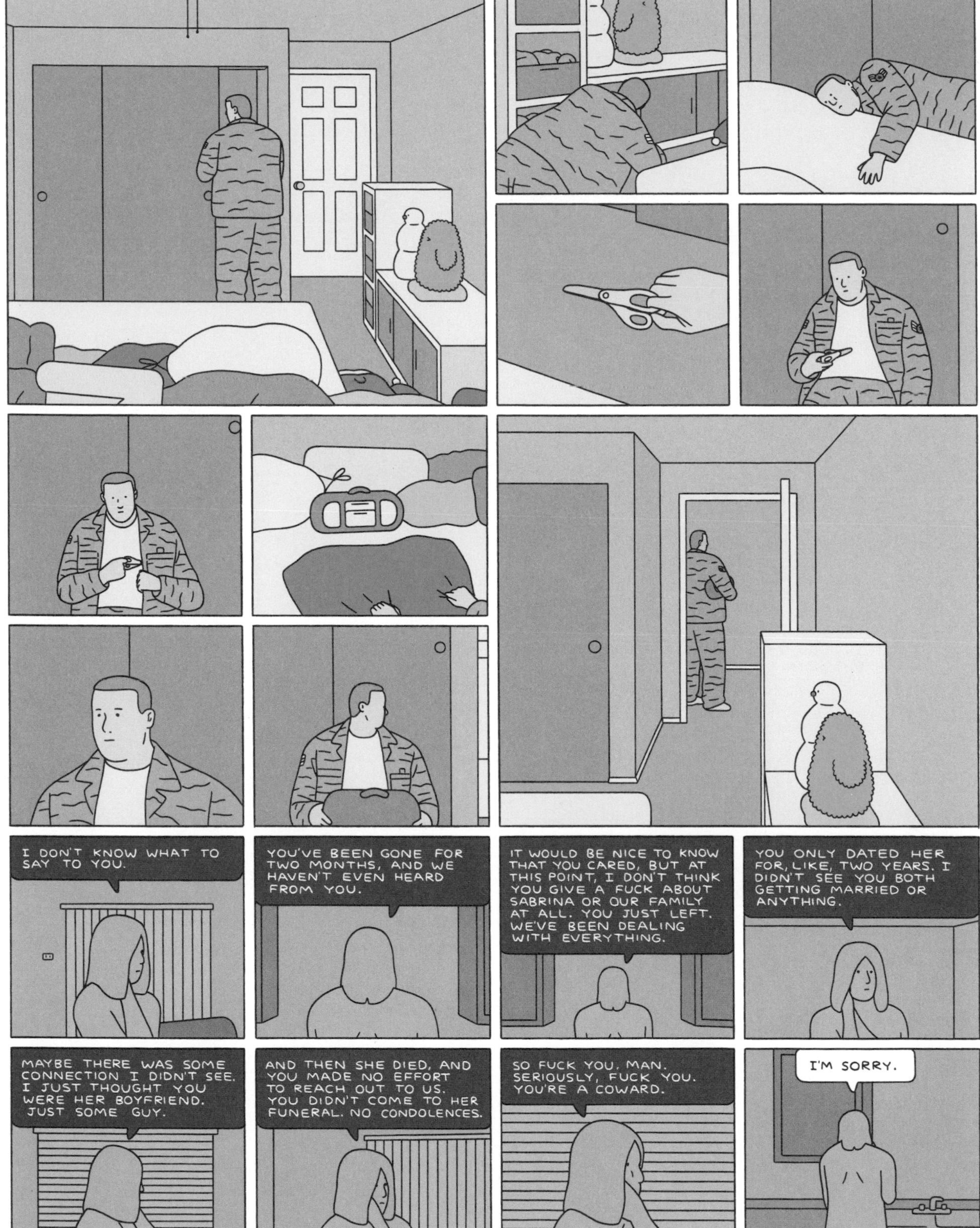
I DON'T KNOW WHAT TO SAY TO YOU.
YOU'VE BEEN GONE FOR TWO MONTHS, AND WE HAVEN'T EVEN HEARD FROM YOU.
IT WOULD BE NICE TO KNOW THAT YOU CARED, BUT AT THIS POINT, I DON'T THINK YOU GIVE A FUCK ABOUT SABRINA OR OUR FAMILY AT ALL. YOU JUST LEFT. WE'VE BEEN DEALING WITH EVERYTHING.
YOU ONLY DATED HER FOR, LIKE, TWO YEARS. I DIDN'T SEE YOU BOTH GETTING MARRIED OR ANYTHING.
MAYBE THERE WAS SOME CONNECTION I DIDN'T SEE. I JUST THOUGHT YOU WERE HER BOYFRIEND. JUST SOME GUY.
AND THEN SHE DIED, AND YOU MADE NO EFFORT TO REACH OUT TO US. YOU DIDN'T COME TO HER FUNERAL. NO CONDOLENCES.
SO FUCK YOU. MAN. SERIOUSLY, FUCK YOU. YOU'RE A COWARD.
I'M SORRY.

I DON'T REALLY NEED YOU IN MY LIFE AT ALL, TO BE HONEST.
YOU CAN SEND US A CHRISTMAS CARD WITH YOUR FUTURE WIFE IF YOU FEEL LIKE IT, BUT WE'RE NOT FAMILY. I DON'T WANT TO KNOW YOU.
I'M SO SORRY.
JUST THINK ABOUT WHAT I'VE SAID. IT'S BEEN VERY DIFFICULT OVER HERE. WE COULD HAVE SUPPORTED EACH OTHER.
YEA. I JUST WANTED TO TELL YOU THAT.
ALL RIGHT.
TAKE IT EASY.
YOU TOO.

I'VE GOTTA GO. DO YOU WANT ANYTHING SPECIAL FOR DINNER?
NO.

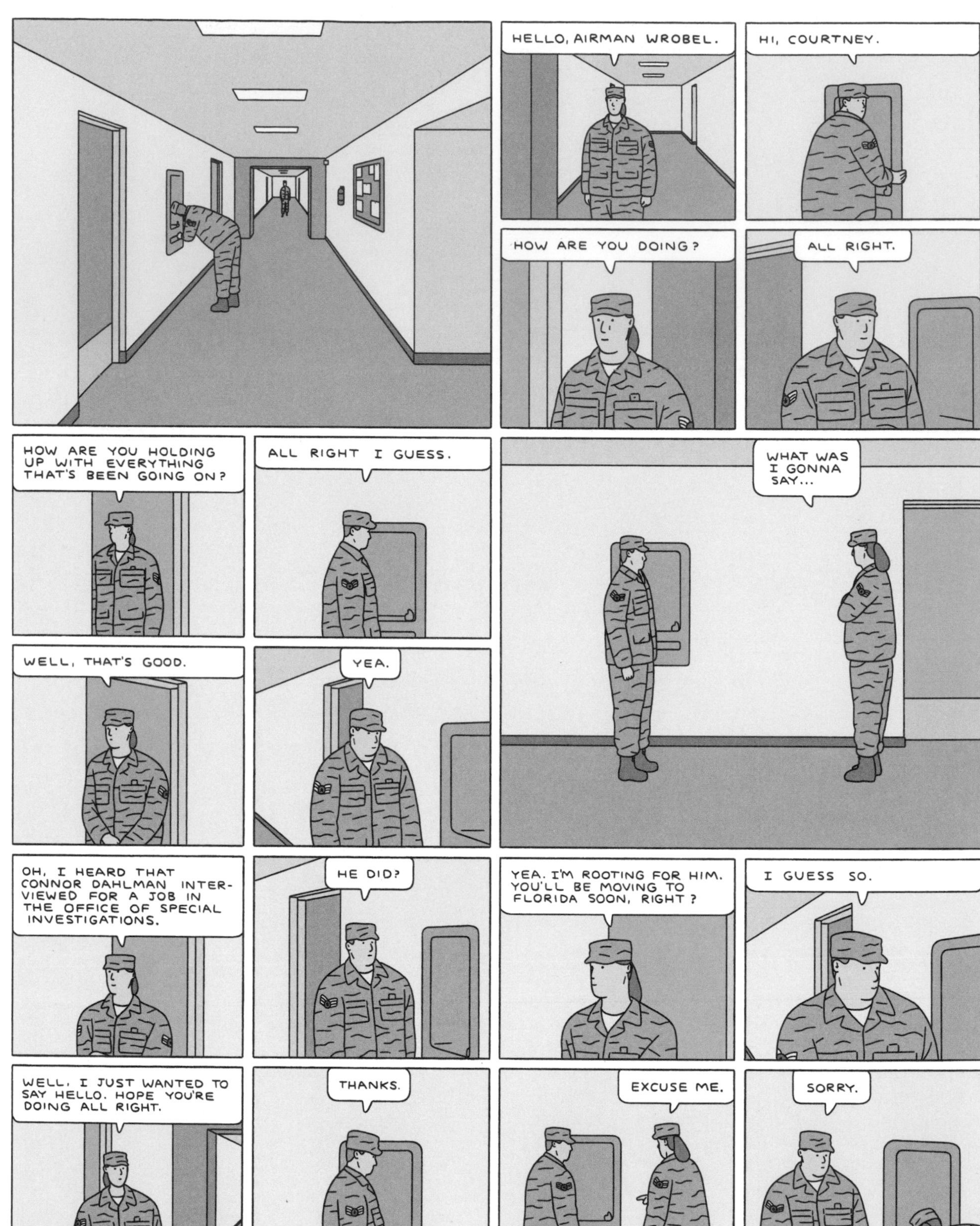
HELLO, AIRMAN WROBEL.
HI, COURTNEY.
HOW ARE YOU DOING?
ALL RIGHT.
HOW ARE YOU HOLDING UP WITH EVERYTHING THAT'S BEEN GOING ON?
ALL RIGHT I GUESS.
WHAT WAS I GONNA SAY...
WELL, THAT'S GOOD.
YEA.
OH, I HEARD THAT CONNOR DAHLMAN INTER-VIEWED FOR A JOB IN THE OFFICE OF SPECIAL INVESTIGATIONS.
HE DID?
YEA. I'M ROOTING FOR HIM. YOU'LL BE MOVING TO FLORIDA SOON, RIGHT?
I GUESS SO.
WELL, I JUST WANTED TO SAY HELLO. HOPE YOU'RE DOING ALL RIGHT.
THANKS.
EXCUSE ME.
SORRY.

HEY, SIMON.
HEY.
HOW ARE YOU DOING?
GOOD.
WE SHOULD GET TO-GETHER SOMETIME. WE HAVEN'T DONE THURS-DAY DINNER IN A LONG TIME.
YEA, WE SHOULD.
YEA.

COMPOSE

Inbox (631)

Starred

Important

Sent Mail

Drafts

Good News

Jason Richmond 4:50 PM
to me

Hey Calvin!

Read this article I found. Fascinating stuff! I hope you've been thinking about what I wrote to you last night.

Your friend,
Truth Warrior

One-thousand miles south of Hawaii lies the US-controlled Palmyra Atoll.

Once used as a naval station during World War II, it has mostly been privately owned, until the year 2000, when the Nature Conservancy purchased Palmyra for thirty-million dollars.

Since then, small research teams have inhabited Palmyra on a rotating basis. There are no permanent residents or significant infrastructure. All the roads that were created by the Navy have overgrown and become unusable. That's the simple story of this forgotten tropical paradise.

This is not the truth.

The atoll is actually a "black site," used by the US government as a secret prison. I know this because I've been there.

I was on a flight from Los Angeles to Sydney, Australia, falling in and out of sleep, drowsy from my medication. I awoke to an announcement. We had to make an emergency landing at an airstrip south of Hawaii. Through later research, I surmised that this could have only been Palmyra Atoll.

I felt sick and asked to be taken off the plane. The air smelled good and the water was clear. Little animals scurried about. To my surprise, we came upon a community of clean, well-dressed English speakers. They appeared to be well cared for and in good spirits.

I asked what they were doing there and this is what I was told.

They were all abducted under similar circumstances. Few seemed to understand why they were targeted, but the general feeling was that the US government and the CIA were somehow behind their captivity.

I was told that, among the inhabitants, there was an entire classroom of children and a subway train of strangers that found themselves kidnapped, hooded, and dropped on the atoll. Their captors gave no explanation, and they've never received news from the outside world.

Upon arrival, they are vaccinated and tested for diseases. They are sterilized to control the population. They are told that those who choose to cooperate will live out their days in isolated bliss, wanting for nothing, working for no one. Those who refuse are summarily executed.

New captives are shaken and frightened, but welcomed warmly by the small community. They are never abused in the adjustment process, simply allowed to adapt peacefully to their new reality.

They are not under lock and key. There is no supervision. There are no guards. So far as I could tell, there are no laws put in place by the captors. It seems that the community succeeds or fails by its own moral code.

They don't behave like prisoners. There is no hierarchy. No one is in charge or superior to anyone else. They didn't even ask to leave or help them escape or send word to their families. One man said he had been there for forty years.

I was told that many happy couples have found love on the compound. They live in comfortable, small wooden homes. There are generators for refrigeration and light. Food is delivered regularly, and a doctor visits once a month.

Books are sometimes dropped off as well, and a small library has been amassed. Most of them seem to have come from public libraries in the American Midwest, where I'm from. There was a book from my hometown library. I checked the circulation card and found the name of my third grade teacher.

I asked a teenage girl if there was a message she wanted to send back to civilization. She said "no."

We were back in the air within an hour, this strange encounter a foggy memory as I drifted back to sleep.

I've tried to revisit the colony, but charter flights are not allowed to land on the air strip. Officially, the atoll is used exclusively as a conservation research center, but I know the truth.

Now, when I see an atrocity unfold on the news, I wonder if the victims are bound and gagged on a flight to Palmyra. It would not surprise me if the dead at Sandy Hook, the Boston Marathon, and Sabrina Gallo were now living together, totally unaware of the impact they are having on the world.

It leaves me to wonder. Maybe, as I write this, Sabrina Gallo sits in the sand, watching the sunset. Maybe she'll walk back to the common area where people gather for dinner and play cards under generated light. Maybe she will outlive all of us. It helps me sleep to consider these pleasant scenarios.

I hope you believe that I mean what I say.

I am writing a book about my experience on Palmyra Atoll that will be self-published in the spring of 2018. Donations and pre-orders are welcomed and greatly appreciated. ▫

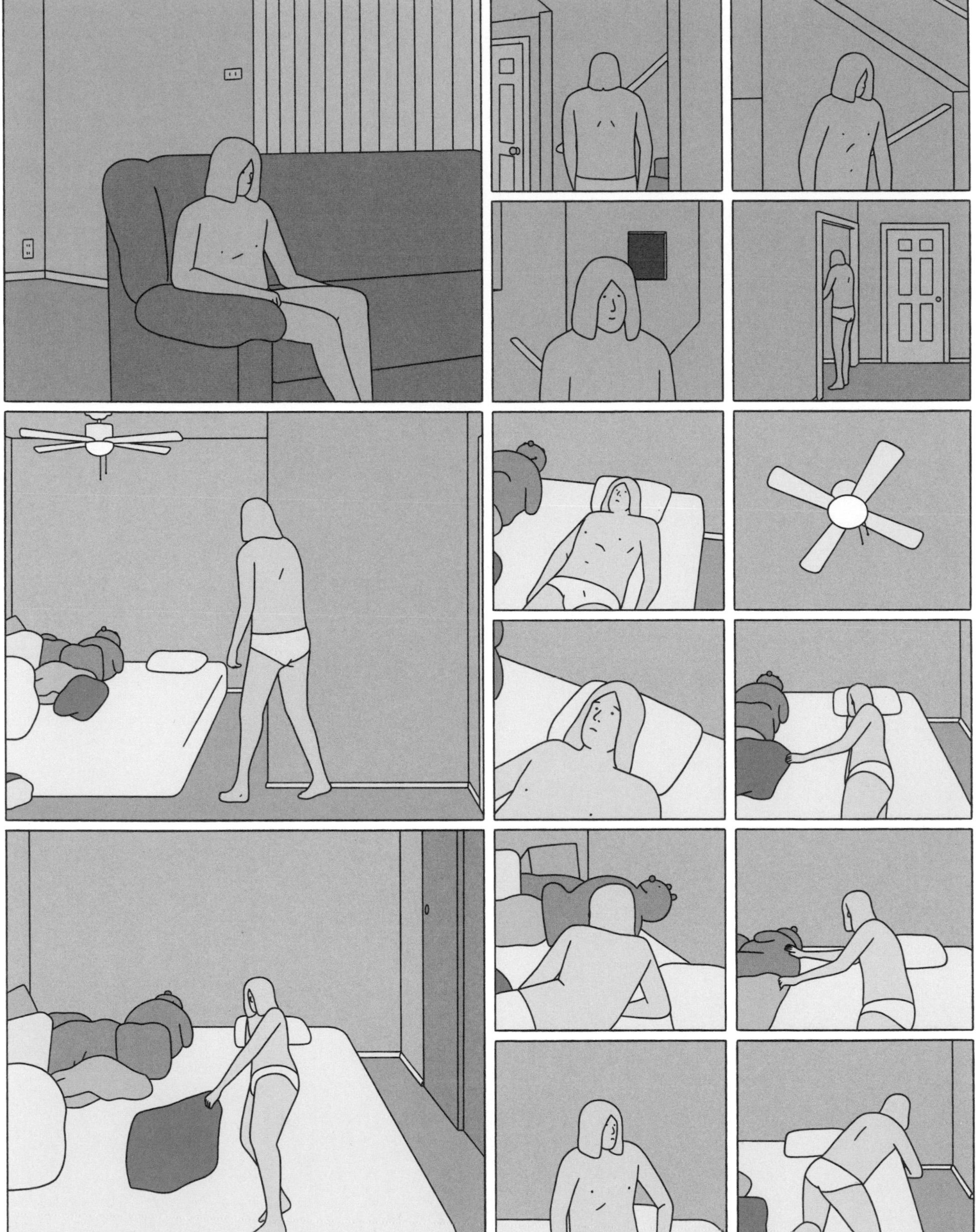

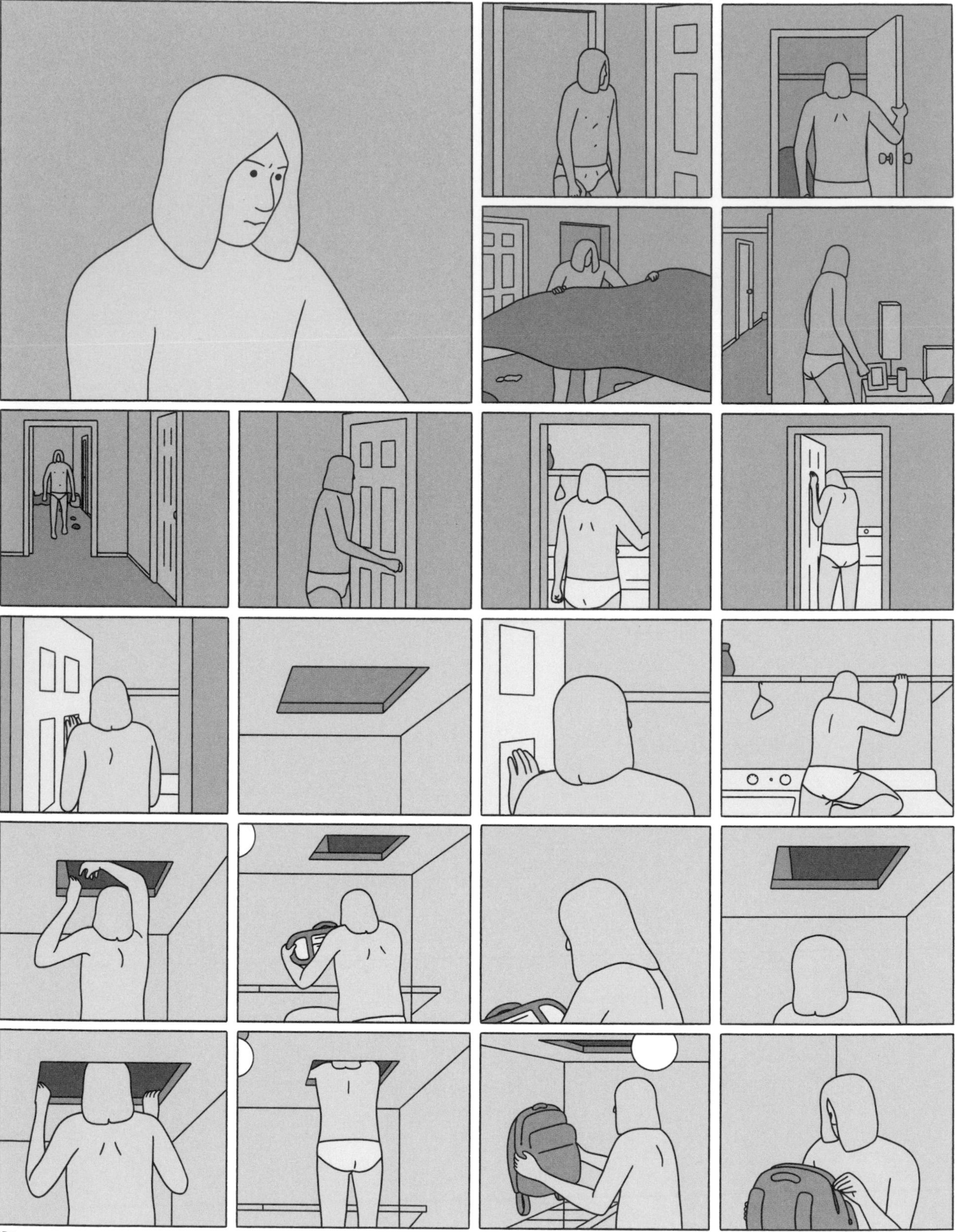

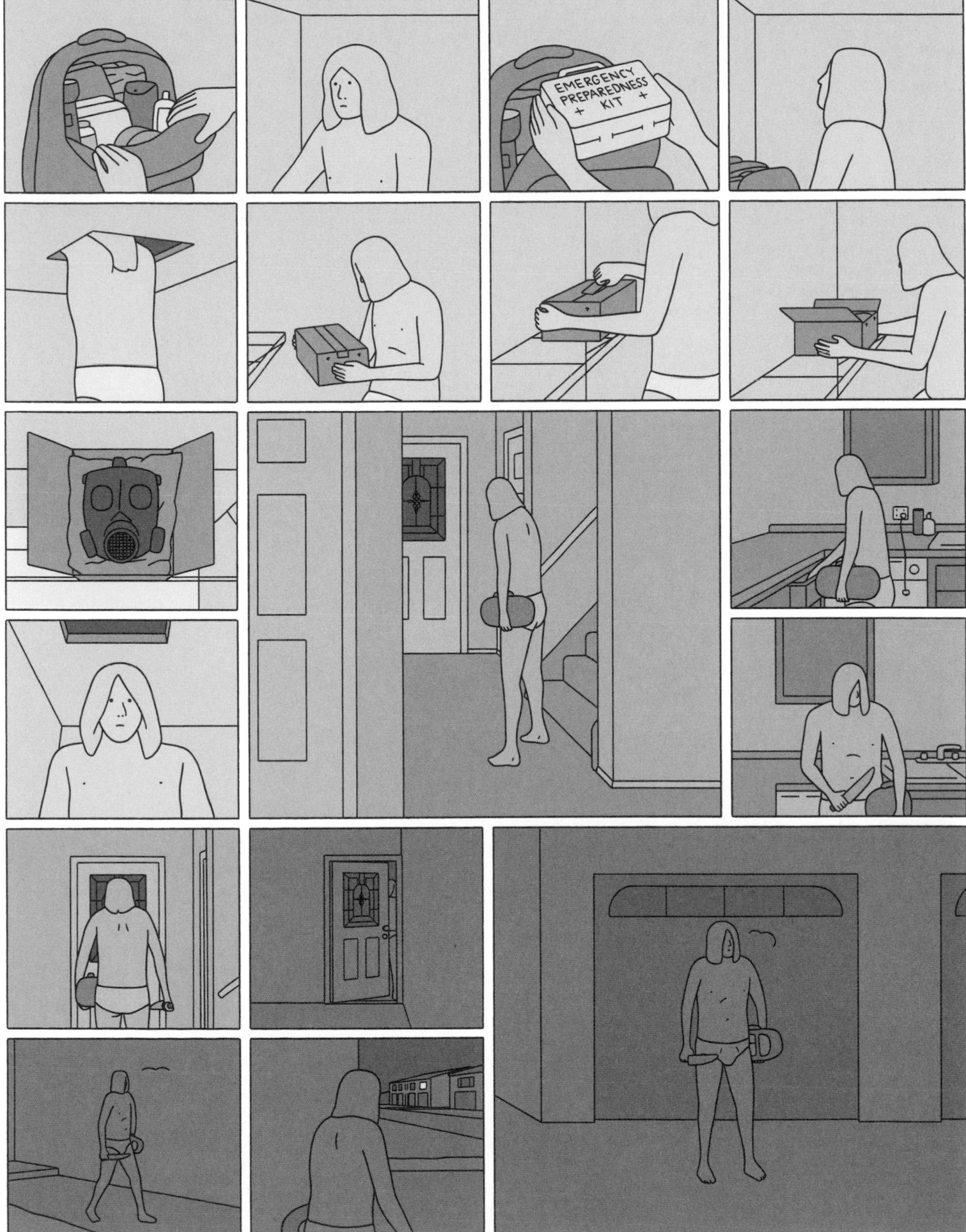
EMERGENCY
PREPAREDNESS
+ KIT +

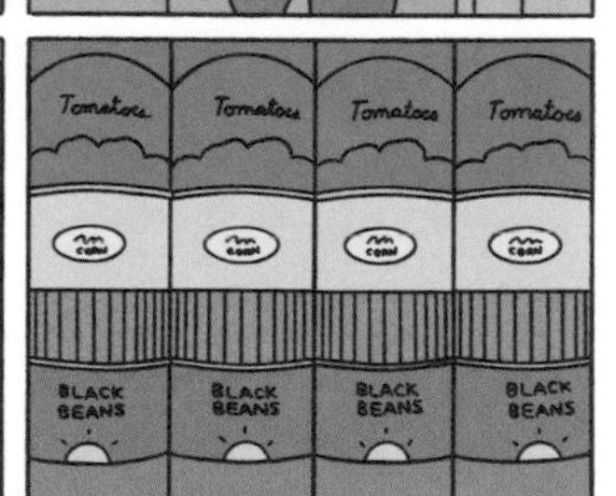
Tomatoes
Tomatoes
Tomatoes
Tomatoes
BLACK BEANS
BLACK BEANS
BLACK BEANS
BLACK BEANS
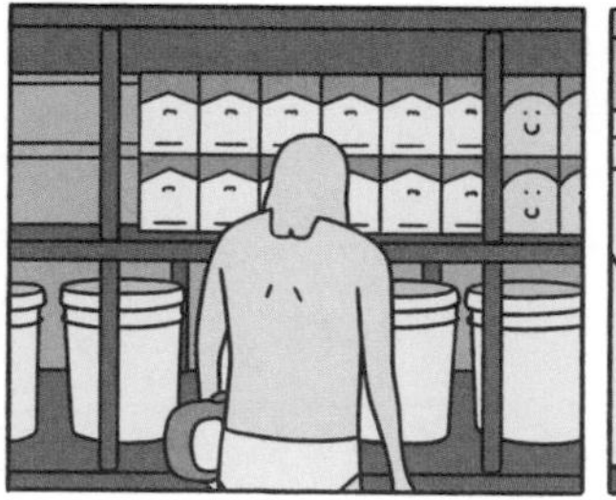

FOOD-PREP
305 Servings
1 MONTH

THIS IS IT, MY FRIENDS. I CAN'T BELIEVE WE ARE EACH GIVEN ONE LIFE AND IT HAS TO COME TO THIS. IT IS TRULY A WASTE AND A TRAGEDY.

I WISH YOU ALL THE BEST, BUT THERE'S NOTHING I CAN DO TO HELP YOU AFTER TONIGHT. I FEEL I'VE BEEN A SELFLESS AND RIGHTEOUS PATRIOT, BUT AT A CERTAIN POINT I MUST PROTECT MYSELF AND MY OWN. I HOPE YOU'VE HEEDED MY COUNTLESS WARNINGS, AND YOU'RE WELL-PREPARED.

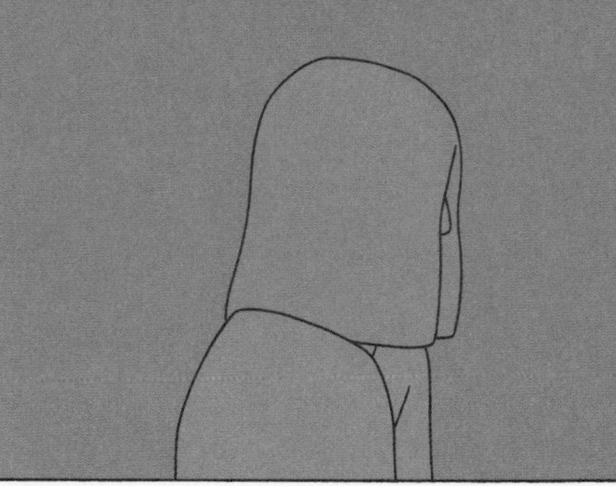

I HAVE IT FROM A SOURCE IN A HIGH PLACE THAT THE TROOPS ARE MOBILIZED, UNDER THE GUISE OF A DEFENSIVE DRILL. THIS IS NOT SOME WORST-CASE SCENARIO PREDICTION. THEY ARE COMING FOR US NOW. RIGHT NOW. I'VE BEEN SCREAMING ABOUT THIS FOR FIFTEEN YEARS.

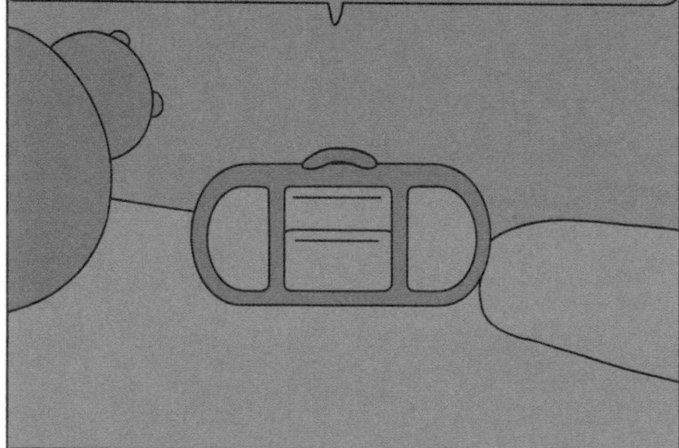

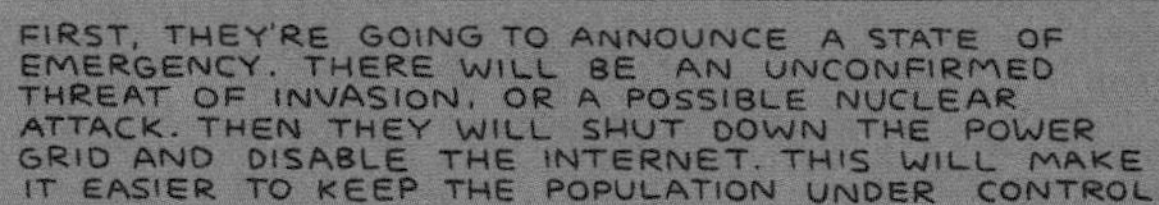

FIRST, THEY'RE GOING TO ANNOUNCE A STATE OF EMERGENCY. THERE WILL BE AN UNCONFIRMED THREAT OF INVASION, OR A POSSIBLE NUCLEAR ATTACK. THEN THEY WILL SHUT DOWN THE POWER GRID AND DISABLE THE INTERNET. THIS WILL MAKE IT EASIER TO KEEP THE POPULATION UNDER CONTROL.

THEN THEY WILL HALT FOOD TRANSPORTATION. THINK ABOUT WHAT WILL HAPPEN WHEN YOUR GROCERY STORE SHELVES ARE EMPTY. WHERE WILL YOU TURN? THIS IS WHEN THEY WILL ESTABLISH RALLYING POINTS FOR FOOD AND SUPPLIES.

THEN YOU WILL HAVE FRIGHTENED AND DEFENSELESS GROUPS OF PEOPLE BEING SHEPHERDED TOGETHER, AND THEY WILL BE COMPLETELY DEPENDENT ON THOSE IN CONTROL. GAME OVER. THE MOMENT TO ORGANIZE AN ARMED REBELLION HAS PASSED.

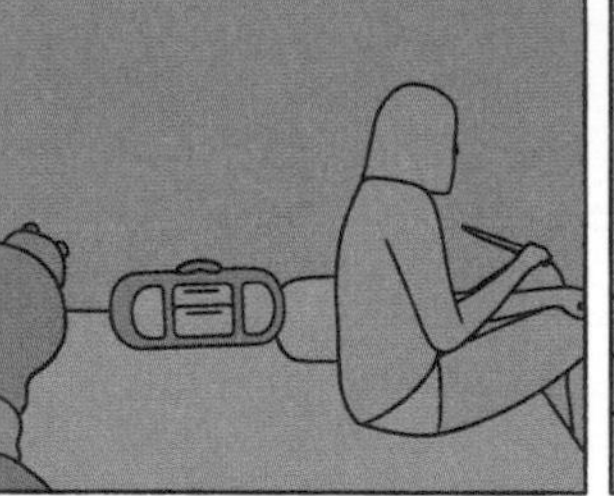

I'VE EXPOSED REPORTS ABOUT THE NEED TO REDUCE THE GLOBAL POPULATION BY EIGHTY PERCENT BY THE YEAR TWENTY-TWENTY. THIS COULD VERY WELL BE THAT MOMENT OF RECKONING.

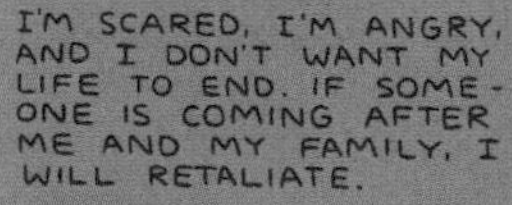

I'M SCARED, I'M ANGRY, AND I DON'T WANT MY LIFE TO END. IF SOMEONE IS COMING AFTER ME AND MY FAMILY, I WILL RETALIATE.

I'M SORRY, BUT I THINK I'M GOING TO HAVE TO CUT THE BROADCAST SHORT. I HAVE A LOT TO DO TONIGHT. FOR THE REST OF THE SHOW I'VE PREPARED A PLAYLIST OF MY FAVORITE SONGS FROM MY YOUTH. I HOPE YOU ENJOY IT. GOOD LUCK.

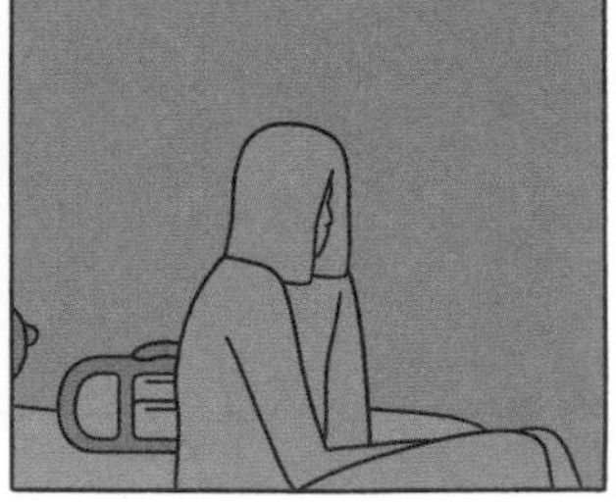

FORTY-FOUR DEGREES IN COLORADO SPRINGS. SUNNY SKIES. ZERO PERCENT CHANCE OF SNOW THE REST OF THE DAY.
LOOKING AT TRAFFIC, WE HAVE AN ACCIDENT SOUTHBOUND ON I-25, CAUSING DELAYS BE-TWEEN FILLMORE AND FONTANERO.
HOPE YOU'RE HAVING A LOVELY DAY. YOU'RE LISTENING TO KCCP. NOW A WORD FROM OUR SPONSORS.
RUNNING ERRANDS.
THERE IS SOME FOOD IN THE FRIDGE.
BE HOME AFTER WORK W/ MORE GROCERIES.

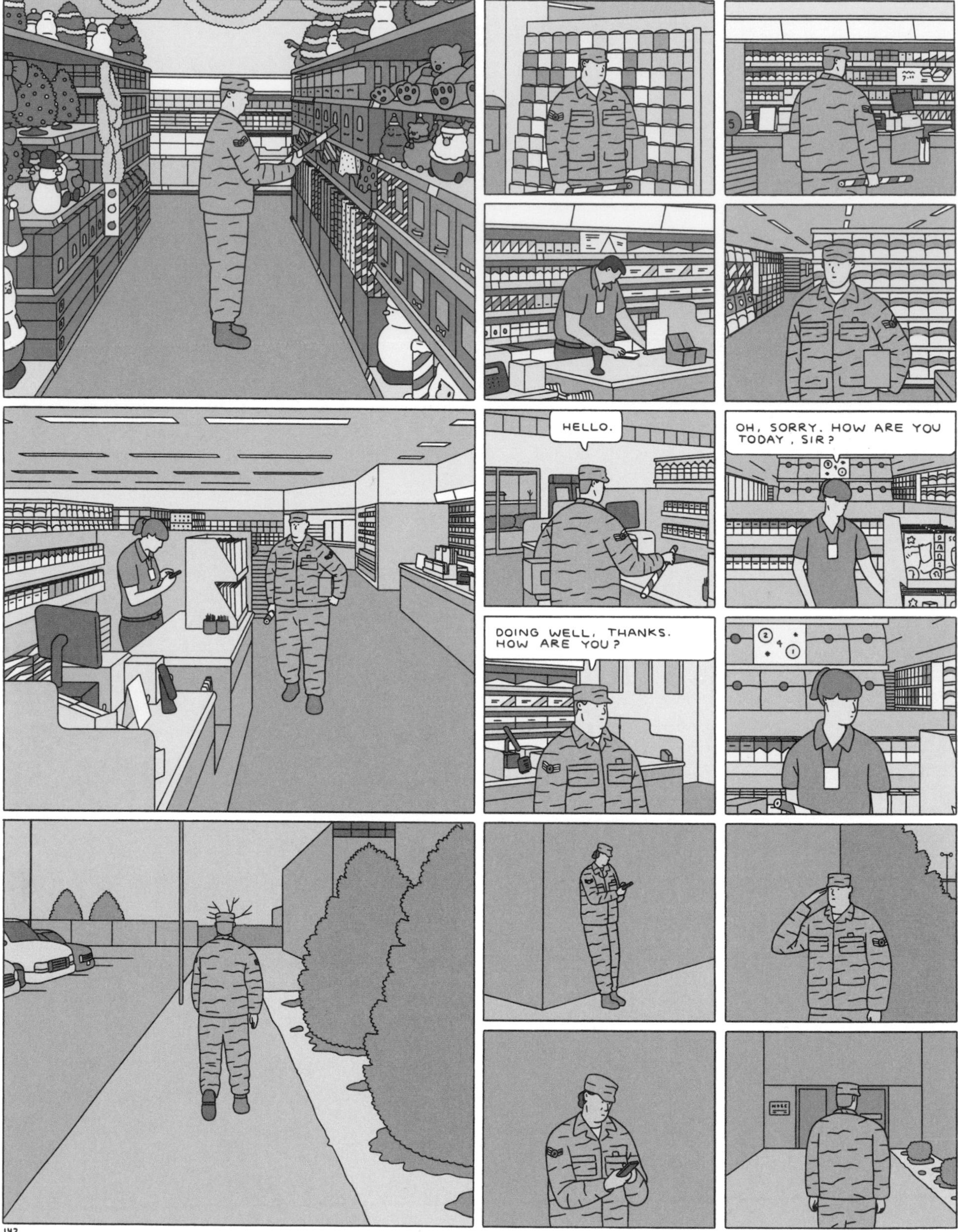
HELLO.
OH, SORRY. HOW ARE YOU TODAY, SIR?
DOING WELL, THANKS. HOW ARE YOU?

WHAT'S GOING ON?

WHAT'S WRONG?

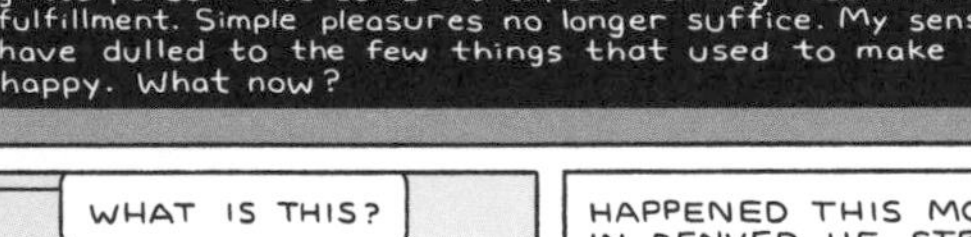
>>What about me?! Everyone tells me I am a supremely gifted person. I've come to expect nothing less than total fulfillment. Simple pleasures no longer suffice. My senses have dulled to the few things that used to make me happy. What now?

>>What am I supposed to do, live an unappreciated life and be forgotten forever? Where is my parade? I have to express myself somehow. If it can't be positive, it will have to be negative. All that matters is I'm remembered.

WHAT IS THIS?

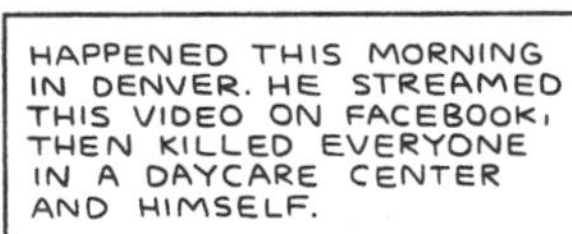
HAPPENED THIS MORNING IN DENVER. HE STREAMED THIS VIDEO ON FACEBOOK, THEN KILLED EVERYONE IN A DAYCARE CENTER AND HIMSELF.

GOD.

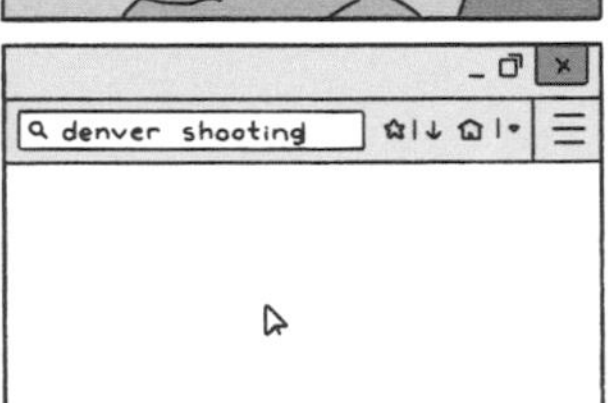
denver shooting

Denver Massacre - No Survivors
NOT CROSS POLICE LINE DO NOT CROSS

First victim identified as teacher Nancy Sullivan:

DOD MEDICAL EVALUATION REVIEW BOARD
MENTAL HEALTH SURVEY
PETERSON AIR FORCE BASE COLORADO

DATE: 11/10/17
NAME: SrA Calvin Wrobel

How many hours of sleep did you receive last night?	2-4 ○	4-6 ●	6-8 ○	8-10 ○	10-12 ○
How many alcoholic beverages did you consume last night?	0 ○	1 ●	2 ○	3 ○	4+ ○
Rate your overall mood from 1 to 5, 1 being poor:	1 ○	2 ○	3 ●	4 ○	5 ○
Rate your stress level from 1 to 5, 5 being severe:	1 ○	2 ○	3 ●	4 ○	5 ○
Are you experiencing depression or thoughts of suicide?	Y ○	N ●			

If yes, elaborate: ________

Is there anything in your personal life that is affecting your duty?	Y ○	N ●

If yes, elaborate: ________

Would you like to speak with a clinical psychologist?	Y ○	N ●

Additional Comments: ________

WELL, LISTEN, SOMETIMES YOU HAVE TO RUN WITH THE INFORMATION YOU RECEIVE. I STILL TRULY BELIEVE THAT SOMETHING EVIL IS IN MOTION. IT'S JUST A MATTER OF TIME. I THOUGHT YESTERDAY COULD HAVE BEEN THE MOMENT OF TRUTH.
IT'S GOOD, THESE FALSE ALARMS. WAKING UP WITH EVERYTHING AT PEACE AND RETURNED TO NORMAL MAKES ME THANKFUL TO BE ABLE TO FIGHT ANOTHER DAY. LET THAT BE A LESSON TO YOU ALL TO BE BETTER PREPARED IN THE FUTURE.
ON TO BUSINESS: DENVER. LET'S TALK ABOUT IT. ANOTHER BIG ONE. YOUNG TODDLERS. THE FINAL DEATH TALLY IS AT THIRTY-ONE.
MORE OF THE SAME. THE GLOBALISTS WILL STOP AT NOTHING TO UNDO OUR CONSTITUTIONAL RIGHTS.
I'M SICK OF THESE--

Aa 	Bb 	Cc 	Dd 	Ee 	Ff 	Gg 
Hh 	Ii 	Jj 	Kk 	Ll 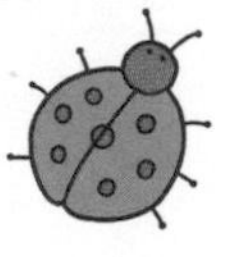	Mm 	Nn 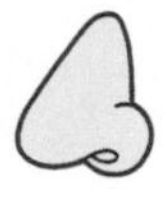
Oo 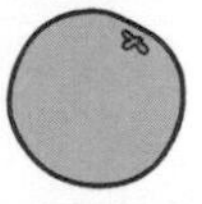	Pp 	Qq 	Rr 	Ss 	Tt 	Uu 
Vv 	Ww 	Xx 	Yy 	Zz 		

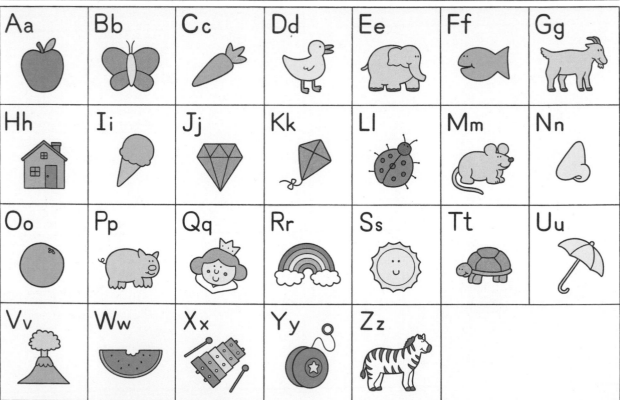

SPOT THE DIFFERENCES

CAN YOU FIND ALL TWENTY DIFFERENCES IN THESE TWO PICTURES?

Lion: This isn't working.

Squirrel: Nonsense! Watch how Miss Mouse dances.

Miss Mouse: 1... 2... 3... 4...

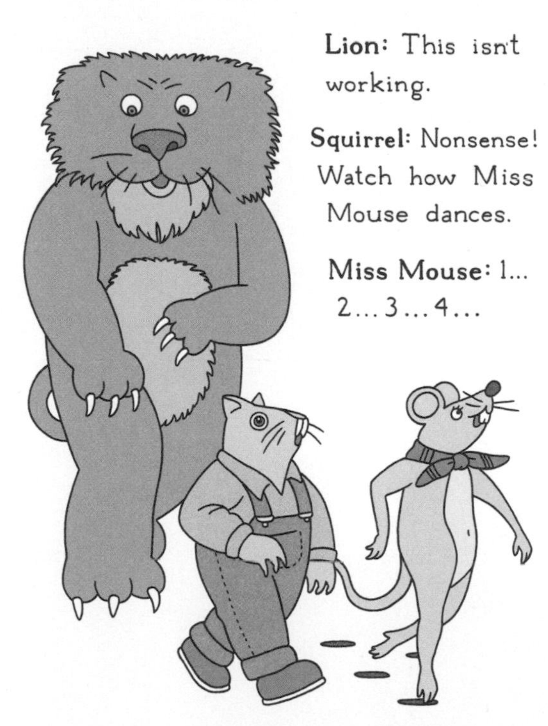

Lion: 1... 2... It's no use!

Miss Mouse: We won't judge you. Don't be afraid to get silly.

Tiger: Watch me!

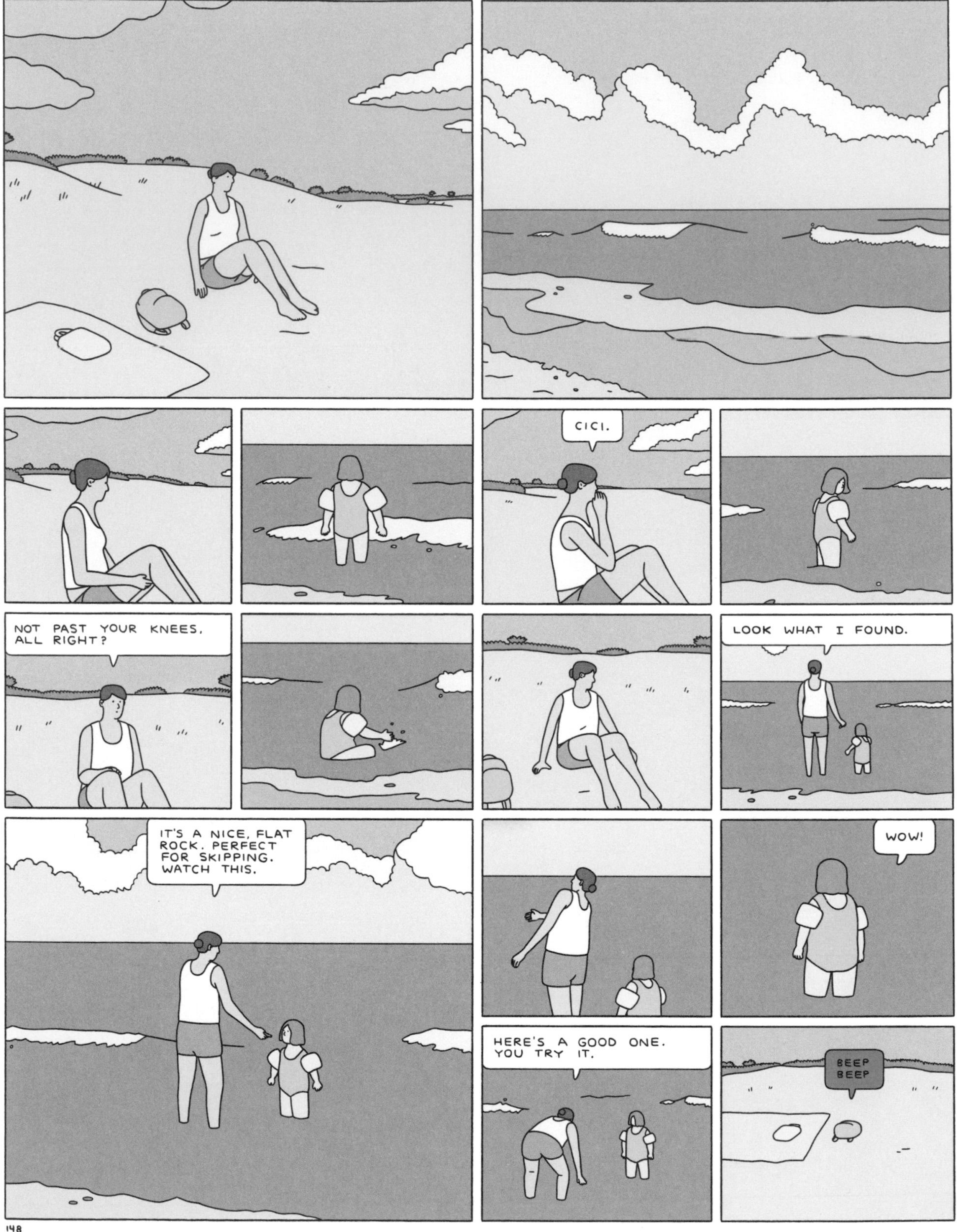
CICI.
NOT PAST YOUR KNEES, ALL RIGHT?
LOOK WHAT I FOUND.
IT'S A NICE, FLAT ROCK. PERFECT FOR SKIPPING. WATCH THIS.
WOW!
HERE'S A GOOD ONE. YOU TRY IT.
BEEP BEEP

I'M GONNA ANSWER THAT. BE CAREFUL.
HEY.
WE'RE DOING WELL. HOW ARE YOU?
GOOD. HOW IS YOUR FRIEND DOING?
LET ME KNOW IF THERE'S ANYTHING I CAN DO.
APARTMENT HUNTING? WHEN WERE YOU THINKING OF COMING OUT HERE?
I DON'T KNOW. I'LL HAVE TO CHECK MY WORK SCHEDULE.
NO, IT'S FINE.
WHEN IS YOUR LAST DAY?
WOW. ONLY A FEW MONTHS AWAY.
CAN I CALL YOU WHEN I GET HOME TONIGHT AND WE CAN TALK ABOUT IT?
YOU TOO.

ALL RIGHT. HAVE A GOOD DAY.

SORRY ABOUT THAT.

NO PROBLEM. IS EVERY-THING OK?

OH, YEA. JUST WANTED TO CHECK IN WITH JACKIE.

SO, DO YOU FEEL LIKE YOU'VE MADE THE RIGHT CHOICE?

YOU KNOW WHAT, I DO. I'M LOOKING FORWARD TO BEING A REGULAR PERSON AGAIN.

I LIKE FLORIDA. AND I MISS MY DAUGHTER AND JACKIE.

THINGS ARE STARTING TO CALM DOWN. IT'S BEEN A TERRIBLE YEAR, BUT WE GOT THROUGH IT.

YOU CAN SAY THAT AGAIN.

WHAT LOOKS GOOD?

I'D LOVE A CLUB SANDWICH.

ME TOO.

Sandra,
I'll be home from work at 9. Please have some left-over pasta.
Love,
Mom

HARDW

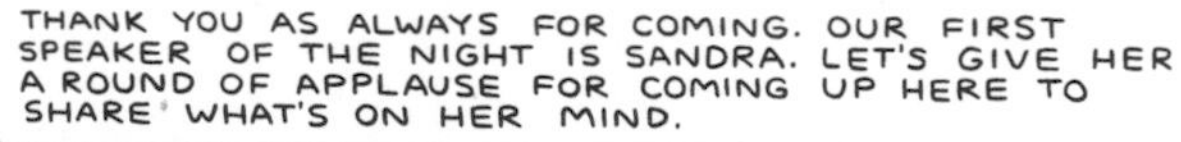
THANK YOU AS ALWAYS FOR COMING. OUR FIRST SPEAKER OF THE NIGHT IS SANDRA. LET'S GIVE HER A ROUND OF APPLAUSE FOR COMING UP HERE TO SHARE WHAT'S ON HER MIND.

THANKS.

UM... I'M GOING TO READ SOME THINGS...

MY SISTER WAS KILLED RECENTLY.

SINCE THEN, I'VE BEEN GETTING THESE MESSAGES FROM ALL OVER THE PLACE.

IF IT'S ALL RIGHT, I WAS JUST GOING TO READ SOME FROM DIFFERENT STRANGERS.

I DON'T WANT TO MAKE ANY-ONE UNCOMFORTABLE. I HOPE THIS IS OK.

OK. HERE THEY ARE.

"HEY SANDRA. MY HEART IS BREAKING FOR YOU AND YOUR FAMILY. WHAT CAN I DO? WHERE CAN I SEND A DONATION?"

"IS THIS SANDRA GALLO'S OFFICIAL E-MAIL? WRITE ME BACK. I THINK I MAY HAVE INFORMATION THAT WILL BE USEFUL TO YOU."

"SANDRA. WHAT IS GOING ON? THIS JUST DOESN'T ADD UP."

"HI SANDRA. I SENT YOU A MESSAGE ON FACEBOOK. WHAT'S UP? IS THIS FOR REAL OR WHAT? I THINK YOU OWE US AN EXPLANATION."

"IS THIS REALLY YOUR E-MAIL ADDRESS? WHAT PROOF DO WE HAVE THAT YOUR IDENTITY IS REAL, JUST LIKE YOUR FAKE SISTER?"

"I'VE BEEN STUDYING PICTURES OF YOU AND YOUR SISTER ONLINE, AND THERE SEEMS TO BE A DIS-CREPANCY BETWEEN YOUR HAIR COLOR AND THE SHAPE OF YOUR NOSE BEFORE JUNE OF LAST YEAR. HOW CAN YOU EXPLAIN THIS?"

"SANDRA. THE COMMUNITY NEEDS TO KNOW THE TRUTH. THE INCONSISTENCIES HAVE BECOME IMPOSSIBLE TO IGNORE. IF YOU DON'T STEP FORWARD AND EXPLAIN YOURSELF, WE WILL NEED TO TAKE THE NEXT STEP. THIS INJUSTICE CANNOT STAND."

"HI SANDRA. I'M A PHOTOGRAPHER BASED IN MILWAUKEE. I FIND YOUR SADNESS QUITE BREATH-TAKING, AND WOULD LOVE TO SHOOT YOU FOR A SERIES I'M WORKING ON. LET ME KNOW IF THERE'S A PLACE WE CAN MEET UP NEXT WEEK."

"HEY. I SAW YOUR PICTURE IN THE NEWSPAPER. IF I SENT YOU THE CLIPPING, WOULD YOU BE ABLE TO SIGN IT FOR ME?"

"HEY SANDRA. I HAVE REASON TO BELIEVE YOUR SISTER IS STILL ALIVE. I DON'T KNOW YOUR INVOLVEMENT IN THE STORY, IF YOU ARE REAL OR WHAT, BUT I THOUGHT YOU WOULD WANT TO KNOW. MESSAGE ME FOR DETAILS."

UM, I'M GONNA SKIP SOME OF THESE. THIS LAST PERSON HAS BEEN SENDING ME DEATH THREATS.

THIS IS WHAT HE SAID: "YOUR ADDRESS IS ONLINE. PEOPLE IN OUR COMMUNITY ARE WAKING UP TO THE TRUTH. I'M ARMED AND PROTECTED. SEE WHAT HAPPENS IF THEY TRY AND TEST ME.

"I DON'T BUY THIS STORY. I DON'T REALLY BELIEVE ANYTHING I'M TOLD FROM SO-CALLED VERIFIED SOURCES. REMEMBER THE GULF OF TONKIN? WHY SHOULD WE BELIEVE YOUR STORY?

"THIS WHOLE THING IS FAKE. IT'S A FUCKING LIE. IT DOESN'T MAKE ANY SENSE. WHERE IS SHE?"

I THINK THAT'S ALL I WANT TO READ.

I'M SORRY. I DON'T KNOW IF THIS WAS THE RIGHT THING TO DO.

THANKS.

THANK YOU, SANDRA.

WHY DON'T WE TAKE A BREAK FROM THE READING AND HAVE A MOMENT OF SILENCE.

HOW ARE YOU FEELING? DO YOU FEEL ANY BETTER?
NOT REALLY.

KITTY?

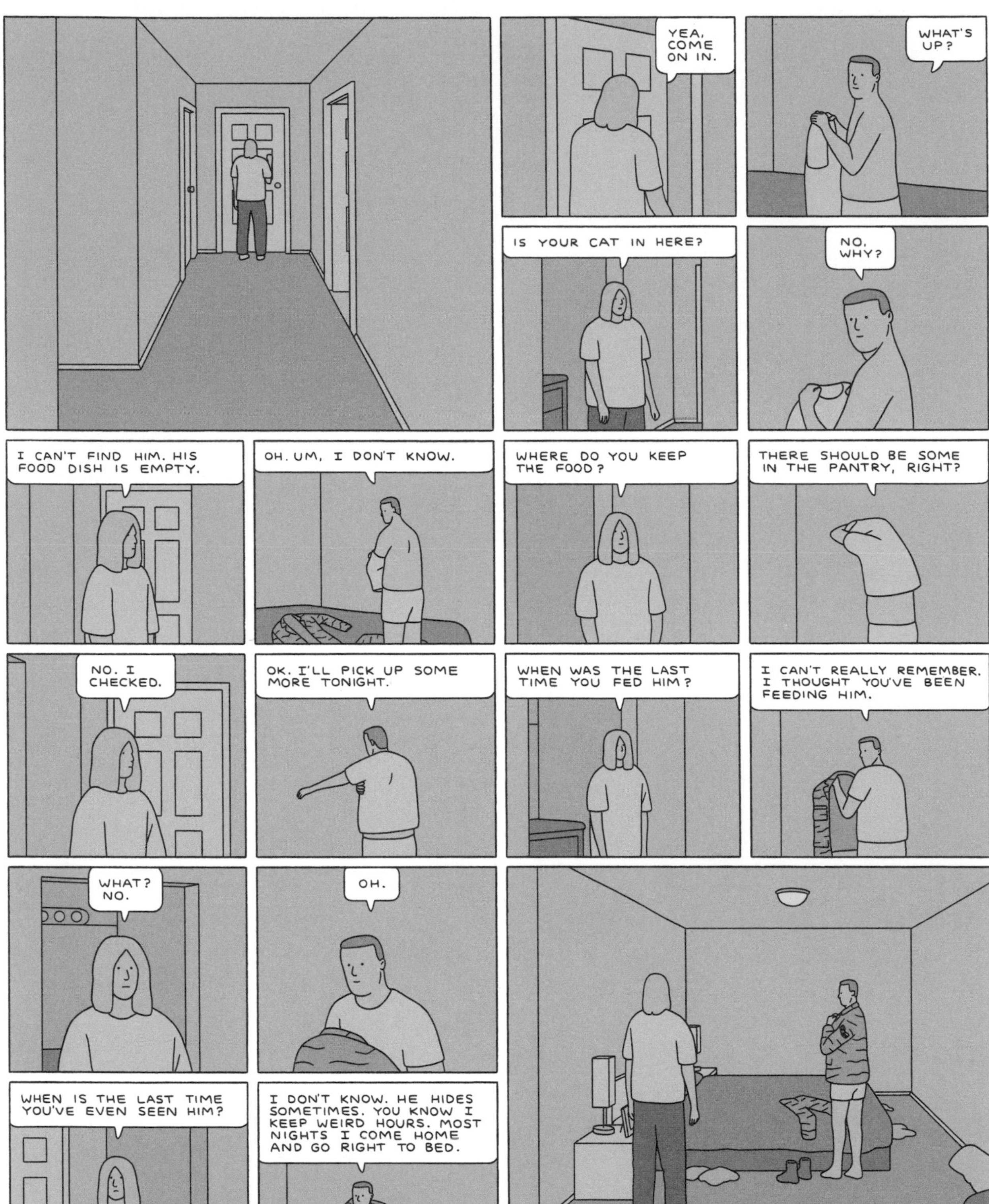
YEA, COME ON IN.
WHAT'S UP?
IS YOUR CAT IN HERE?
NO, WHY?
I CAN'T FIND HIM. HIS FOOD DISH IS EMPTY.
OH. UM, I DON'T KNOW.
WHERE DO YOU KEEP THE FOOD?
THERE SHOULD BE SOME IN THE PANTRY, RIGHT?
NO. I CHECKED.
OK. I'LL PICK UP SOME MORE TONIGHT.
WHEN WAS THE LAST TIME YOU FED HIM?
I CAN'T REALLY REMEMBER. I THOUGHT YOU'VE BEEN FEEDING HIM.
WHAT? NO.
OH.
WHEN IS THE LAST TIME YOU'VE EVEN SEEN HIM?
I DON'T KNOW. HE HIDES SOMETIMES. YOU KNOW I KEEP WEIRD HOURS. MOST NIGHTS I COME HOME AND GO RIGHT TO BED.

HE MUST BE AROUND HERE SOME-WHERE.
I'LL KEEP LOOKING.
OK. JUST LET ME FINISH GETTING READY.
ANY LUCK?
NO.
OH.
DO YOU LET HIM OUTSIDE?
NO. NEVER.
I MEAN, MAYBE I WAS HAVING A SMOKE ON THE PORCH AND HE SLIPPED OUT. IT'S POSSIBLE.
SO, WHAT ARE WE GOING TO DO?
WELL, I REALLY HAVE TO GO TO WORK.
SHOULDN'T WE GO OUT AND LOOK FOR HIM?
YEA...BUT I REALLY CAN'T RIGHT NOW. IT'S JUST BAD TIMING.

ARE YOU SERIOUS?
I'LL GO OUT THEN.

I USED UP ALL MY SICK DAYS FOR THE YEAR. I JUST CAN'T DO IT.

THAT'S IT?

MY HANDS ARE TIED. I PROMISE I'LL PUT UP SIGNS TOMORROW.

THAT'S A GOOD IDEA.

CAN I TAKE THESE WINTER CLOTHES?

OF COURSE.

IT'S COLD OUT THERE.

YEA.

I'M SURE HE'LL TURN UP.

ALL RIGHT.

READY?

WELL, CALL ME IF YOU FIND HIM.

OK.

UM, HERE.

TAKE TEN BUCKS. YOU MIGHT NEED IT. BUY YOURSELF DINNER.
WHAT IS THE CAT'S NAME?
OH. IT'S, UH, RANDY.
ALL RIGHT, MAN. GOOD LUCK.
RANDY!

RANDY!

HAVE YOU SEEN A BLACK CAT? LIKE A DARK GRAY CAT?

SORRY, I HAVEN'T. WHERE DO YOU LIVE?

MY FRIEND LIVES RIGHT AROUND THE CORNER. UH, COULD YOU LOOK UP CALVIN WROBEL IF YOU FIND HIM?

SURE THING. JILL, KEEP AN EYE OUT, ALL RIGHT?

I WILL.

THANKS.
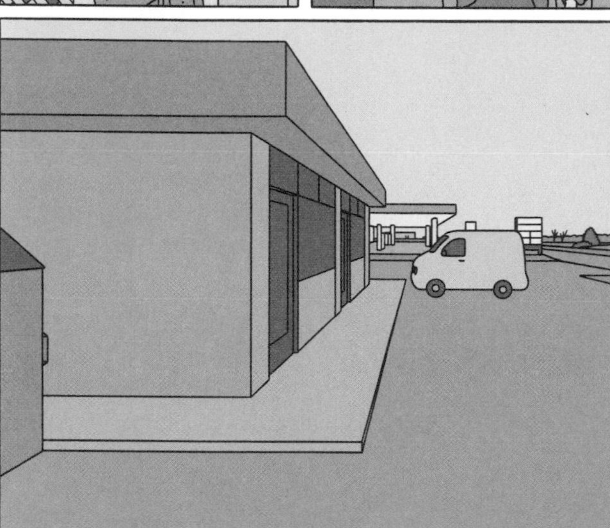

RANDY!

WHAT'S WRONG?

HAVE YOU SEEN A CAT?
YOU KNOW WHAT, I SAW A LITTLE GRAY CAT WALKING AROUND ON CHELTON. THIS WAS YESTERDAY, THOUGH.

THIS WAY?

YEA. NEAR ACADEMY BOULEVARD. IT'S WORTH A SHOT.

THANKS.

RANDY!
DAMMIT.
RANDY!
HOW'S IT GOING. I'LL HAVE A HAM AND CHEESE TO GO. THANKS.

HOW'S IT GOING?

GOOD.

YEP.

HEY, HAVE YOU SEEN A GRAY CAT AROUND?
AH. NO. SORRY, BUDDY. CAN'T SAY I HAVE.

THANKS ANYWAY.

YOU KNOW, THERE'S A RESCUE SHELTER A FEW MILES DOWN THE ROAD.

THANKS. I'LL CHECK IT OUT.

REALLY?

IT'S THAT WAY, ON THE LEFT. I CAN'T REMEMBER WHAT IT'S CALLED, BUT YOU'LL SEE IT.

ARE YOU WALKING?

YEA.

COME ON, I INSIST.

LISTEN, I'LL GIVE YOU A RIDE DOWN THERE.

SERIOUSLY, I'M GOING THAT WAY ANYWAY.

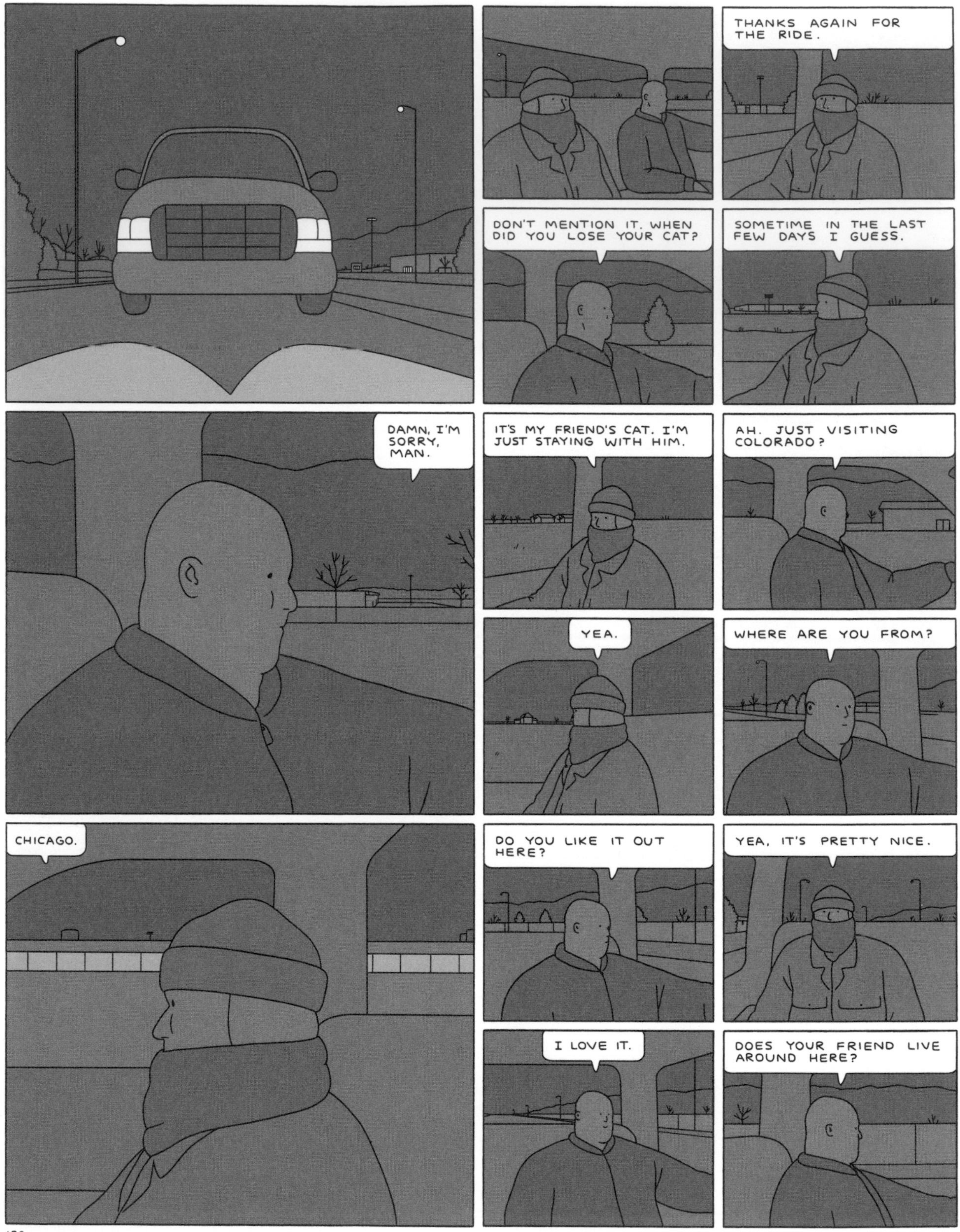
THANKS AGAIN FOR THE RIDE.
DON'T MENTION IT. WHEN DID YOU LOSE YOUR CAT?
SOMETIME IN THE LAST FEW DAYS I GUESS.
DAMN, I'M SORRY, MAN.
IT'S MY FRIEND'S CAT. I'M JUST STAYING WITH HIM.
AH. JUST VISITING COLORADO?
YEA.
WHERE ARE YOU FROM?
CHICAGO.
DO YOU LIKE IT OUT HERE?
YEA, IT'S PRETTY NICE.
I LOVE IT.
DOES YOUR FRIEND LIVE AROUND HERE?

NOT FAR, I THINK.

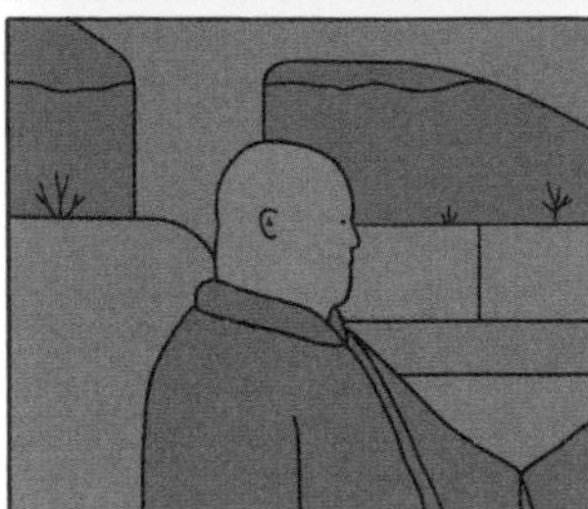

WELL, THANKS. I REALLY APPRECIATE IT.

SURE.

HEY-

HOW ARE YOU GONNA GET HOME?

I CAN WALK BACK.

YOU SURE? I CAN WAIT IF YOU NEED A RIDE.

NO, I DON'T WANT YOU TO DO THAT.

I'VE GOT MY SANDWICH RIGHT HERE. DON'T WORRY ABOUT IT.

WELL, DON'T WAIT TOO LONG FOR ME. YOU REALLY DON'T HAVE TO.

GO, GO. I'LL BE HERE.

HI.
CAN I HELP YOU?
I WAS WONDERING IF SOMEONE BROUGHT IN A GRAY CAT IN THE LAST FEW DAYS.
WE'LL HAVE TO CHECK. I'LL BUZZ YOU IN.
EXIT
HM. THE ONLY GRAY ONE I SEE IS DOWN HERE. IS THIS YOUR GUY?
STAFF
NO. THAT'S NOT HIM.
YEA, I'M SORRY, I DON'T SEE ANYTHING ELSE. I'LL TAKE YOUR NUM-BER AND LET YOU KNOW IF HE SHOWS UP.
STAF
THANKS.
ST
DAMN. NO LUCK?
NO.
WELL, NOW I INSIST ON GIVING YOU A RIDE HOME. I'M THE ONE THAT SENT YOU ON THIS WILD GOOSE CHASE.
ARE YOU SURE?
OF COURSE.

YOU SAID IT'S COMING UP?

YEA. I'M SORRY I CAN'T REMEMBER THE STREET NAME. I'LL KNOW IT WHEN I SEE IT.

SO, HOW LONG WILL YOU BE IN TOWN?

I'M NOT SURE.

WELL, IF I SPOT YOUR CAT, HOW CAN I GET IN TOUCH WITH YOU?

YOU'LL HAVE TO CALL MY FRIEND. OH - MAKE A LEFT HERE.

GOT IT. WHAT'S YOUR FRIEND'S NAME?

CALVIN WROBEL. HE LIVES RIGHT UP HERE. LAST TOWNHOUSE ON THE RIGHT.

THANK YOU SO MUCH FOR YOUR HELP.

MY GOOD DEED FOR THE YEAR. HA HA.

YEA.

DON'T WORRY. I'M SURE THE LITTLE GUY WILL TURN UP.

WELL, HAVE A GOOD NIGHT.

YEA, YOU TOO.

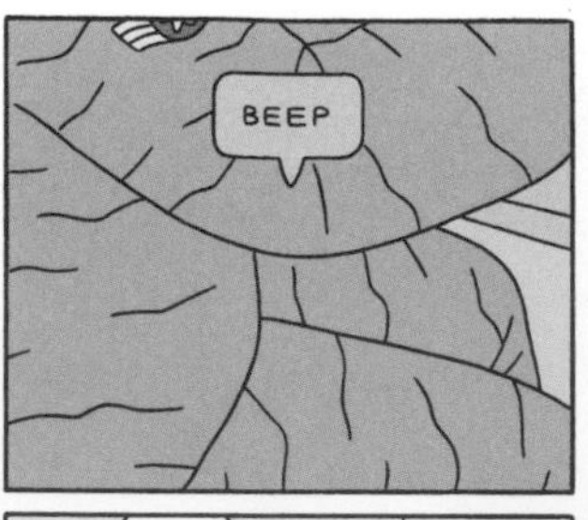
BEEP

SORRY, I'LL BE RIGHT BACK.

HI.

I HOPE YOU'RE HAPPY.

WHAT'S WRONG?

YOUR DAUGHTER IS CRYING RIGHT NOW AND IT'S YOUR FAULT.

WHAT HAPPENED?

DID YOU SEND HER A PACKAGE?

YEA...

A PACKAGE WITH YOUR NAME AND RETURN ADDRESS ON IT.

YEA. WHAT'S WRONG?

AND CHRISTMAS PRESENTS INSIDE THAT SAY "FROM SANTA." NICE GOING, CALVIN.

GODDAMMIT. WHY DID YOU LET HER OPEN IT?

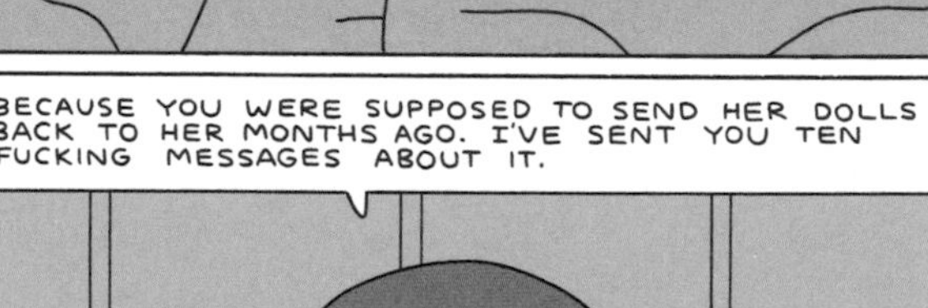

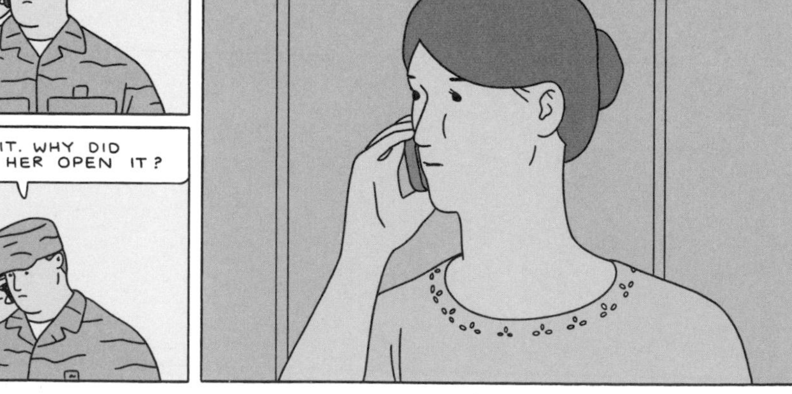
BECAUSE YOU WERE SUPPOSED TO SEND HER DOLLS BACK TO HER MONTHS AGO. I'VE SENT YOU TEN FUCKING MESSAGES ABOUT IT.

I CAN'T BELIEVE THIS. I SENT MY DAUGHTER SOME PRESENTS.

CICI IS BAWLING. SHE'S SCREAMING THAT SANTA ISN'T REAL.

SHE WILL GET OVER IT! SHE'S FOUR YEARS OLD.

LET ME SPEAK TO HER. I'LL APOLOGIZE AND MAKE UP AN EXCUSE. IT WILL BE FINE.

I DON'T WANT YOU TALKING TO HER RIGHT NOW.

I DON'T WANT YOU OUT HERE.

I'M SORRY, ALL RIGHT? IT WAS AN INNOCENT MISTAKE.

I DON'T THINK YOU SHOULD MOVE OUT HERE.

WELL, IT'S TOO LATE NOW.

WE DON'T WANT YOU HERE. CICI DOESN'T EVEN ASK ABOUT YOU ANYMORE.

THAT'S NOT TRUE. I LOVE HER.

YOU CALL ONCE EVERY TWO WEEKS, SOMETIMES IN THE MIDDLE OF THE NIGHT, AND YOU TALK TO HER FOR ABOUT TEN MINUTES.

THAT'S OVER THE PHONE. IT WILL BE DIFFERENT WHEN I'M THERE IN PERSON...

LIKE WHEN WE LIVED IN COLORADO IN THAT HOUSE? WHEN YOU COMPLETELY IGNORED HER? I CAN'T TAKE THAT AGAIN.

LET'S JUST TALK ABOUT THIS LATER. I'M AT WORK.

I'VE SAID EVERYTHING I WANTED TO SAY. I CAN'T STOP YOU FROM MOVING HERE, BUT I DON'T WANT IT.

NEITHER DO YOU. STOP FOOLING YOURSELF.

IS THAT IT?
YEA.
ALL RIGHT. GOODBYE.

SERGEANT SMITH?

OH, HEY, CALVIN.

THIS DAMN THING. I'M TRYING TO GET MY CHIPS.

I NEED TO TALK TO YOU ABOUT SOMETHING.
WHAT'S UP?

I WANT THAT JOB IN THE OFFICE OF SPECIAL INVESTIGATIONS.

SERIOUSLY? IT'S A LITTLE LATE FOR THAT.

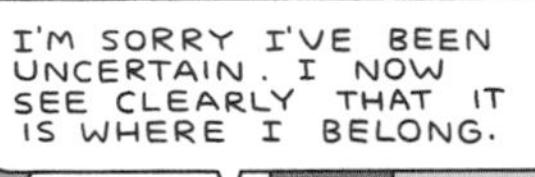
I'M SORRY I'VE BEEN UNCERTAIN. I NOW SEE CLEARLY THAT IT IS WHERE I BELONG.

WELL, I AGREE WITH YOU, BUT DAMN, THE COLONEL HAD TO MOVE DOWN THE LIST WHEN YOU PASSED...

I'M READY. YOU SAID I WAS THE MOST QUALIFIED.

YES, YOU ARE...

YOU HAVEN'T OFFERED ANYONE ELSE THE JOB YET?

NOT YET.

THEN GIVE IT TO ME. I'LL DO ANYTHING.

HM...

LET'S GO UP TO MY OFFICE AND WE'LL FIGURE IT OUT.

THANK YOU, ED. YOU WON'T REGRET THIS.
YEA, I THINK THIS IS RIGHT.
HEY.
HI.
DID YOU FIND HIM?
NO.
DAMN. I'LL LOOK AROUND TOMORROW BEFORE WORK.
WANT A BEER?
NO, THANKS.
ALL RIGHT. I'LL BE UP IN MY ROOM.
OK.

HAVE NOT FORGOTTEN

Jason Richmond 11:35 PM
to me

Calvin Wrobel:

Do I need to introduce myself again? I have been waiting patiently for you to step out of the shadows, but it's clear you have no intention of doing so.

After those 30 kids died, I thought, "OK. Calvin won't sit back and allow this to continue. Any day, he will do the right thing and come forward."

So where are you?

You must have some useful inside knowledge, right? From the Sabrina thing? Just give us a fucking name! This really isn't funny anymore. What kind of monster stands by while children are murdered?

The rest of the world may have forgotten about you, but not me.

A lot of guys only dig into a subject until something new comes along, then they move on to the next big story.

I prefer the more obscure players, people like you, who are on the periphery. Maybe you weren't directly involved, but you can certainly help us uncover who is responsible and bring them to justice.

I just want to help people. Something is clearly out of sorts, can we at least agree on that? You've probably been abused into submission, and my heart goes out to you. These people are so evil, Calvin. I don't think you understand...

Something has to be done. We need you on our side, brother. There is a dark heart at the center of the organization, and I worry that you're getting too close. Set yourself free before it's too late.

What secrets are you hiding? Will you ever blow the whistle? Did they insert a poison capsule into your body that will release if you speak out, or are you just a spineless stooge?

Sometimes I can't believe I'm writing to you, the man whose picture I have analyzed and stared at for days at a time. Do you read this? Will you ever respond to me?

It's just a feeling, but I'm starting to think you are not a good person. No disrespect. Maybe someday you will wake up and do what's right, but until then, you are my sworn enemy.

Give Sabrina my best, you bastard. Let her go. I know you know where she is.

I won't wait for another tragedy to warn you again.

I hate you so much!!!

Always and forever watching you,

Truth Warrior

CALVIN, HELLO.
OH. SORRY.
THERE'S A PROBLEM WITH A SERVER. WOULD YOU MIND CHECKING IT OUT?
NO PROBLEM. WHAT'S WRONG?
I'M GETTING AN ERROR MESSAGE FROM ROW CC, RACK FOUR.
I CAN'T SEEM TO FIGURE IT OUT FROM UP HERE. I'LL NEED YOU TO GO DOWN THERE AND CONSOLE IN.
YOU BET.
THANKS.

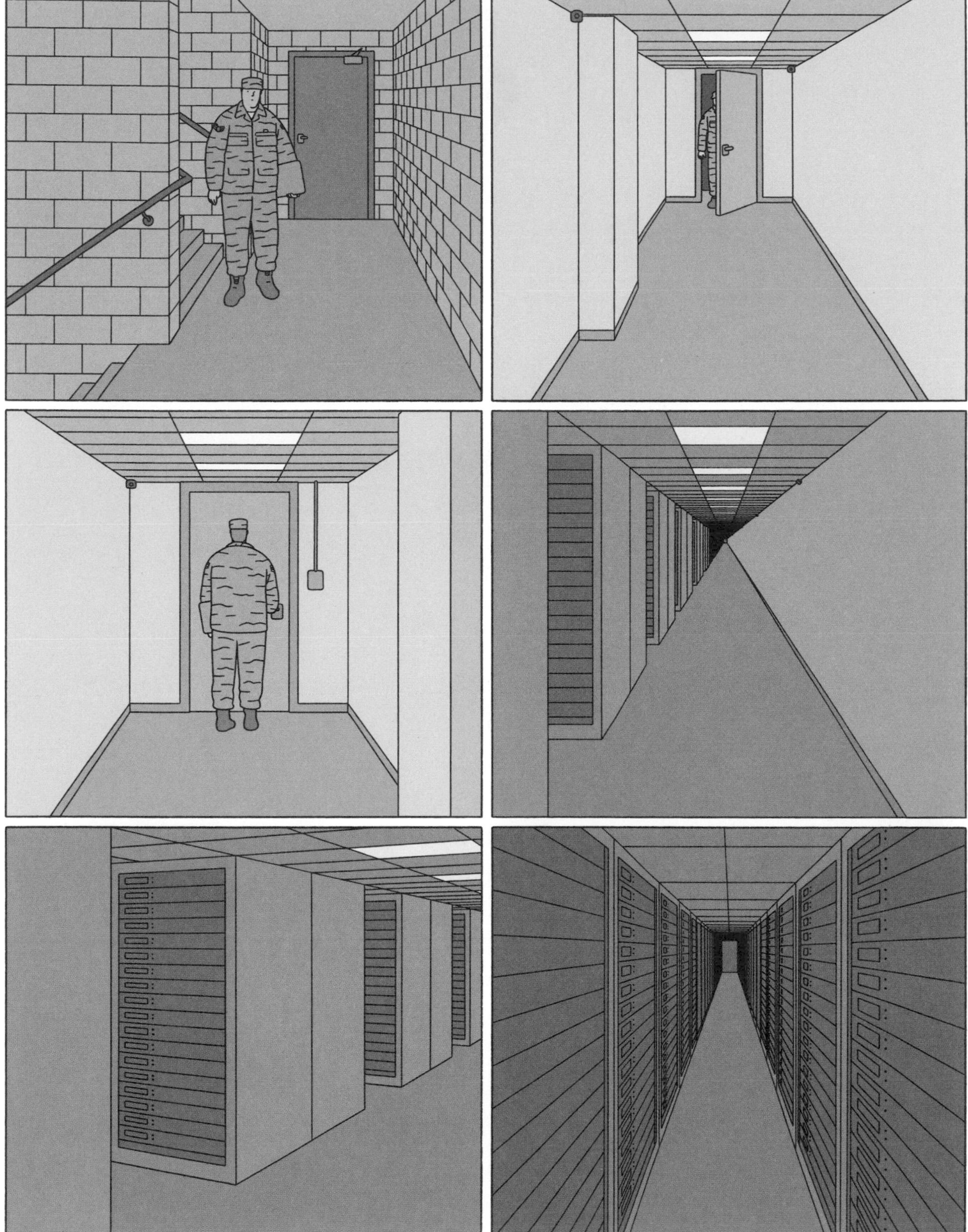

HM.
HEY, CALVIN.

WHOA!

JESUS, CONNOR. HA HA. WHAT ARE YOU DOING DOWN HERE?

I JUST CAME TO SEE IF YOU NEEDED ANY HELP.

OH, NO. I COULDN'T SEEM TO FIND ANYTHING WRONG WITH IT.

OH, GOOD. THAT'S A RELIEF.

YEA.

I WANTED TO TALK TO YOU ABOUT THE JOB...

OK.

AND JUST TELL YOU CONGRATULATIONS, MAN.

OH. THANKS A LOT, CONNOR. I REALLY APPRECIATE IT.

I THINK IT WILL BE GOOD FOR YOU.

WELL, YOU KNOW, IT'S A BIG COMMITMENT. SERGEANT SMITH SAYS A LOT OF MY EXPER-IENCES HERE WILL BE USEFUL THERE.

I JUST HOPE YOU'RE PREPARED.

YEA, YOU KNOW, IT'S A NEW CHALLENGE...

IT IS A BIG COMMIT-MENT.

YEA, I KNOW.

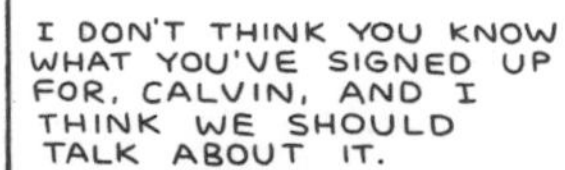
I DON'T THINK YOU KNOW WHAT YOU'VE SIGNED UP FOR, CALVIN, AND I THINK WE SHOULD TALK ABOUT IT.

WHAT DO YOU MEAN?

IT'S NOT LIKE IT IS HERE. YOU WON'T BE SITTING AT A DESK THE WHOLE TIME.

OH, RIGHT. THAT. YOU KNOW, I'M FINE WITH IT. I'M PREPARED TO TRAVEL IF I HAVE TO.

TRAVEL? WHAT ABOUT EXTRA-JUDICIAL KIL-LINGS? ARE YOU PREPARED FOR THAT?

WHAT?

WHAT IF AN AMERICAN CITIZEN NEEDS TO DISAPPEAR, FOR REASONS THAT MIGHT NEVER BE REVEALED TO YOU, AND YOU ARE INVOLVED, EVEN PERIPHER-ALLY, IN THE PLOT? ARE YOU WILLING TO PARTICIPATE IN A CRIME LIKE THAT? SOMETHING THEY CAN HANG OVER YOUR HEAD FOR THE REST OF YOUR LIFE?

THAT'S NOT EVEN THE WORST OF IT, CALVIN. DO YOU READ ABOUT BLACK SITES? YOU KNOW WHAT GOES ON IN THEM, RIGHT? NO, YOU DON'T. NOBODY DOES. ONCE YOU PASS THROUGH THAT DOOR, THERE IS NO LEAVING.

THIS WAS MY CHANCE. I'VE BEEN PREPARING FOR THIS FOR FIVE YEARS. I WAS READY TO GET INSIDE AND FIND OUT FOR MYSELF. YOU THINK YOU'RE GOING TO GERMANY OR SOUTH KOREA TO DO SOME TECH SUPPORT? YOU'VE GOT ANOTHER THING COMING.

CALVIN. YOU DON'T KNOW WHAT THE FUCK YOU'VE GOTTEN YOURSELF INTO. I DON'T THINK YOU HAVE THE STOMACH FOR IT.

WHAT? THAT STUFF IS JUST ANOTHER DAY AT THE OFFICE! I WORRY ABOUT HOW YOU WILL REACT WHEN YOU'RE TAKEN INTO ONE OF THOSE INFAMOUS FALSE FLAG MASSACRES. THAT WORK GETS REALLY HAIRY. WAIT UNTIL YOU MEET THE CRAZY GUYS THEY SEND IN THERE TO PULL THE TRIGGER.

WHAT ABOUT WHEN YOU FIND OUT THINGS THE PUBLIC CAN ONLY DREAM ABOUT? THIS IS LIFE-CHANGING STUFF. WE'RE TALKING ABOUT THE HIDDEN MECHANISMS THAT GOVERN OUR WAKING WORLD. WILL YOUR HEAD EXPLODE UNDER THE PRESSURE?

GODDAMN, MAN. I CAN TELL YOU REALLY HAVE NO CLUE. HA HA. WAIT UNTIL YOU'RE AT THE WATER COOLER AND YOU FIND OUT THE TRUTH ABOUT NINE-ELEVEN. OR WHAT HAPPENED TO SABRINA.

STOP IT! THAT'S ENOUGH!

WHAT? HA HA.

SHUT UP, CONNOR! SHUT THE FUCK UP!

ARE YOU KIDDING ME RIGHT NOW?

I CAN'T TAKE IT!!

DUDE, I AM MESSING WITH YOU.

WHAT?!

CALM DOWN, CALVIN. I'M JOKING AROUND!

YOU DIDN'T REALLY TAKE THAT SER-IOUSLY? COME ON, MAN. YOU'RE SMART-ER THAN THAT.

I MEAN, YEA, I WAS A LITTLE PISSED THAT YOU SWIPED THE JOB FROM ME. KINDA SCREWED UP MY PLANS. I'M JUST GIVING YOU GRIEF.

DAHLMAN

U.S. AIR FORCE

YOU-

JESUS, MAN, YOU'RE PARANOID.

YOU'LL DO GREAT. I MEAN IT. EVERYTHING WILL BE FINE.

SORRY, I'M JUST-

DON'T WORRY ABOUT IT. YOU'VE HAD A STRESSFUL YEAR. YOU GOTTA LEARN TO TAKE A JOKE AGAIN, LIKE YOU USED TO!

YEA...

JUST TAKE IT EASY.

OK. SORRY.

I SHOULD GET BACK UPSTAIRS. SEE YOU THERE?

I'LL BE RIGHT UP.

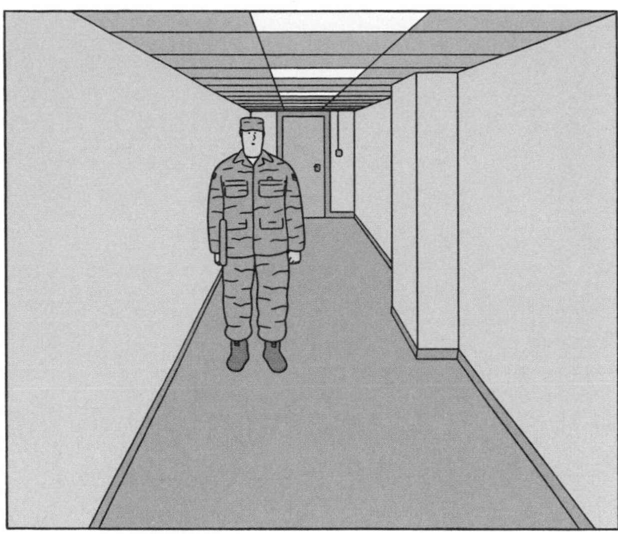

DOD MEDICAL EVALUATION REVIEW BOARD
MENTAL HEALTH SURVEY
PETERSON AIR FORCE BASE COLORADO

DATE: 12/8/17
NAME: SrA Calvin Wrobel

How many hours of sleep did you receive last night?	2-4 ○	4-6 ○	6-8 ●	8-10 ○	10-12 ○
How many alcoholic beverages did you consume last night?	0 ●	1 ○	2 ○	3 ○	4+ ○
Rate your overall mood from 1 to 5, 1 being poor:	1 ○	2 ○	3 ○	4 ○	5 ●
Rate your stress level from 1 to 5, 5 being severe:	1 ●	2 ○	3 ○	4 ○	5 ○
Are you experiencing depression or thoughts of suicide?	Y ○	N ●			

If yes, elaborate: ______

Is there anything in your personal life that is affecting your duty?	Y ○	N ●

If yes, elaborate: ______

Would you like to speak with a clinical psychologist?	Y ○	N ●

Additional Comments: ______

>>Four months later

CALVIN?

HEY. WHAT'S UP?

I JUST CLEARED OUT THE DOWNSTAIRS BATH- ROOM. YOU SURE YOU TOOK EVERYTHING YOU NEED?

YEA, THANKS. DO YOU WANT THESE POTS?

REALLY? YOU SURE YOU DON'T NEED THEM?

AT THIS POINT IT'S EASIER TO BUY NEW STUFF. I'M JUST TAKING WHAT FITS IN THE VAN.

THANKS, MAN. AWESOME.

CONSIDER IT A HOUSE- WARMING GIFT.

HA, YEA. WE'LL KEEP WHATEVER YOU DON'T WANT.

ALL RIGHT. I THINK I'M DONE DOWN HERE.

YOU'RE LEAVING ALL THIS?

YEA.

LET'S GO UPSTAIRS.

I LEFT YOU A LIST OF NUMBERS IN THE KITCHEN DRAWER. CONDO ASSOCIATION. LANDSCAPING SERVICE.

TRASH PICKUP IS ON THURSDAY. RECYCLING MUST BE LOOSE IN THE BIN, NOT BAGGED.

GOT IT.

OH, NICE.

YEA. NOT TOO BAD.

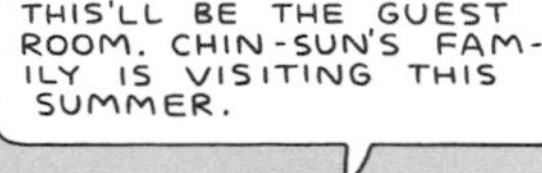
THIS'LL BE THE GUEST ROOM. CHIN-SUN'S FAMILY IS VISITING THIS SUMMER.

NICE LITTLE GUEST BATHROOM HERE.

LET'S TAKE A LOOK AT THE OTHER ROOM.

COOL.

THE CHILD'S ROOM.
HA HA, DON'T EVEN SAY THAT.

NEVER SAY NEVER. EVERYBODY SAYS THAT.

WE'VE TALKED ABOUT IT. I DON'T KNOW...

WELL, I LEFT SOME STUFF BEHIND, JUST IN CASE.

THANKS.

YOU CHECKED OUT THE MASTER BEDROOM ALREADY?

YEP. YOU'RE LEAVING ALL THAT?

MY NEW PLACE IS COMPLETELY FURNISHED. I DON'T NEED ANYTHING.

IS THAT IT, THEN?

THERE'S ROOM FOR THAT BOX DOWN HERE. TURN IT SIDEWAYS. YEA.

WOW, WE DID IT.

WELL, HAVE A SAFE DRIVE. LET ME KNOW WHEN YOU ARRIVE.

I WILL. THANKS AGAIN FOR THE HELP.

SO, WE CAN JUST PAY YOU RENT ON THE FIRST? DOES THAT WORK?

SOUNDS GOOD. LET ME KNOW IF YOU NEED ANYTHING.

ALL RIGHT, MAN. IS THAT IT?

I THINK SO. TAKE CARE, CONNOR.

YOU TOO.

DID YOU CHECK YOUR SPARE TIRE AND YOUR JACK?

YES, DAD.

HA, JUST LOOKING OUT FOR YOU.

THANKS.

ARE WE FOR-GETTING ANY-THING? I THINK THAT'S IT.

OH - WHERE'S THE MAILBOX?

SORRY. THANKS FOR REMINDING ME! IT'S DOWN AT THE END OF THIS COMPLEX.
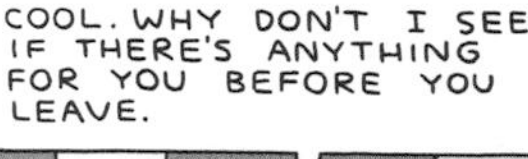

COOL. WHY DON'T I SEE IF THERE'S ANYTHING FOR YOU BEFORE YOU LEAVE.

GOOD IDEA. I ALWAYS FORGET TO CHECK.

BE RIGHT BACK.

GOOD THING I CHECKED.
WOW, THANKS.
I DO EVERYTHING ONLINE NOW. THIS IS ALL JUNK.
CHIN-SUN IS ON HER WAY OVER.
TAKE CARE.
REMEMBER WHAT I TOLD YOU.
WHAT?
HAVE A GOOD TRIP! CALL ME WHEN YOU GET THERE.
OH. SURE THING. SEE YA.

PLAY
HEY!
OH, HEY.
HOW'S IT GOING?
GOOD. I'M GLAD YOU COULD STOP BY. ARE YOU LEAVING NOW?
YEA, PRETTY MUCH. IS THIS A GOOD TIME?
LET ME CHECK.

DORA, WOULD IT BE ALL RIGHT IF I TOOK MY FIFTEEN?
SURE THING.
THANKS.
JUST LET ME WASH MY HANDS.
STAFF
SO I'LL GET AS FAR AS ST. LOUIS TONIGHT, THEN FINISH THE DRIVE TO VIRGINIA TOMORROW.
THAT'S A LONG TRIP.
YEA, I'M EXCITED.
HOW'S THE JOB?
GOOD. EVERY-ONE IS REALLY NICE.
ARE YOU HAPPY OUT HERE?
UM, I DON'T KNOW HOW TO ANSWER THAT. HEH.
YOU'RE RIGHT. SORRY.

DID RANDY EVER TURN UP IN THE SHELTER?
DAMN. POOR LITTLE GUY.

NO.

HAVE YOU TALKED TO SANDRA RECENTLY?

NO.

WELL, I SHOULD GET BACK INSIDE.

OH. SO SOON?

YEA. GOOD LUCK OUT THERE.

THANKS, YOU TOO. HOW CAN I GET IN TOUCH WITH YOU? DO YOU HAVE A PHONE NOW?

YOU CAN JUST CALL THE SHELTER AND ASK FOR ME.

COOL.

THANKS FOR EVERYTHING.

NO PROBLEM.

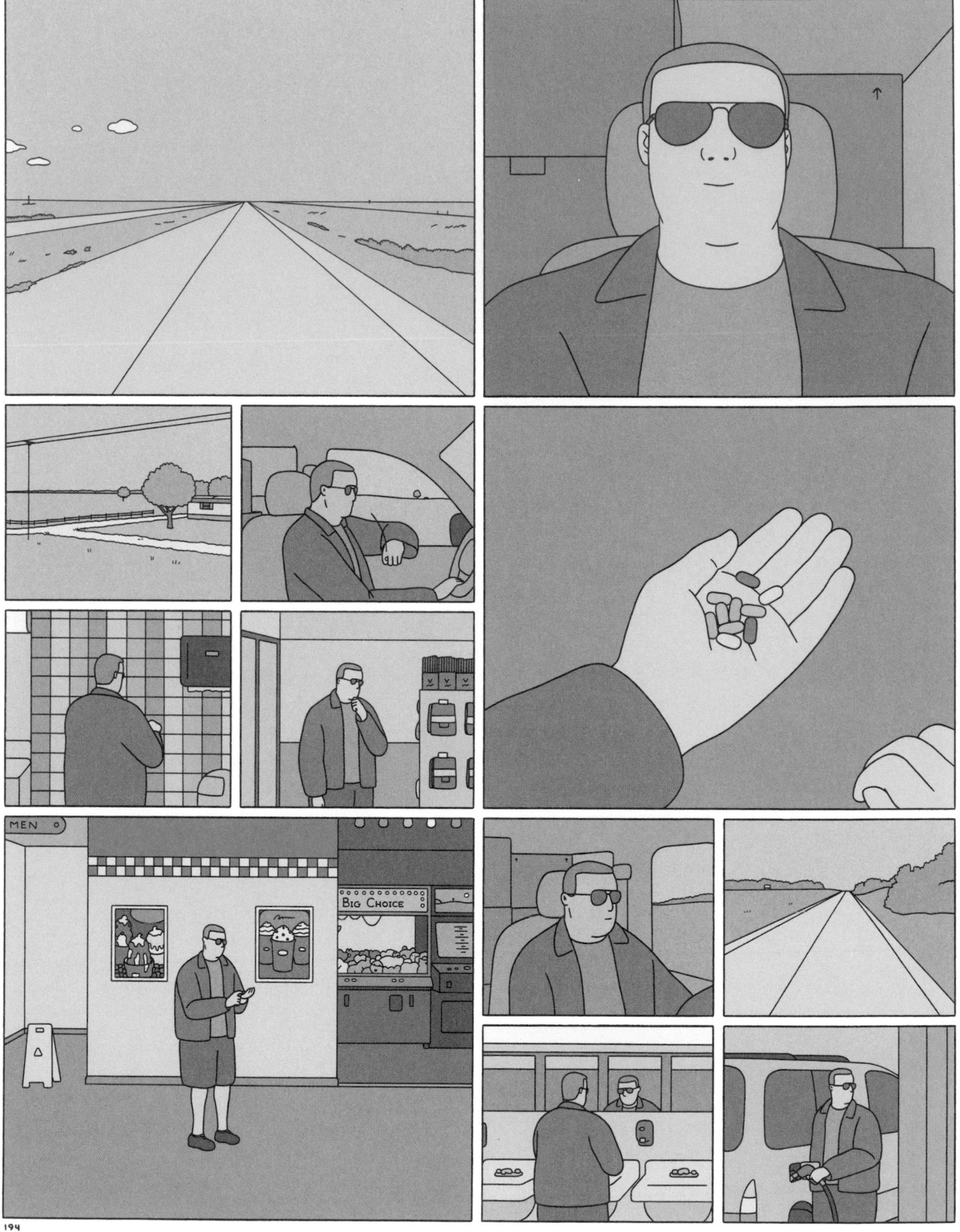
MEN
BIG CHOICE

0%

Do not cross us.
We will always know
where you live.
$5.00 OFF
Your Next Purchase
w/ $25 Min. Purchase
CHICAGO PRODUCE
exp. 6/1/17

LODGING - EXIT 4
8
FOOD - EXIT 4
BB's

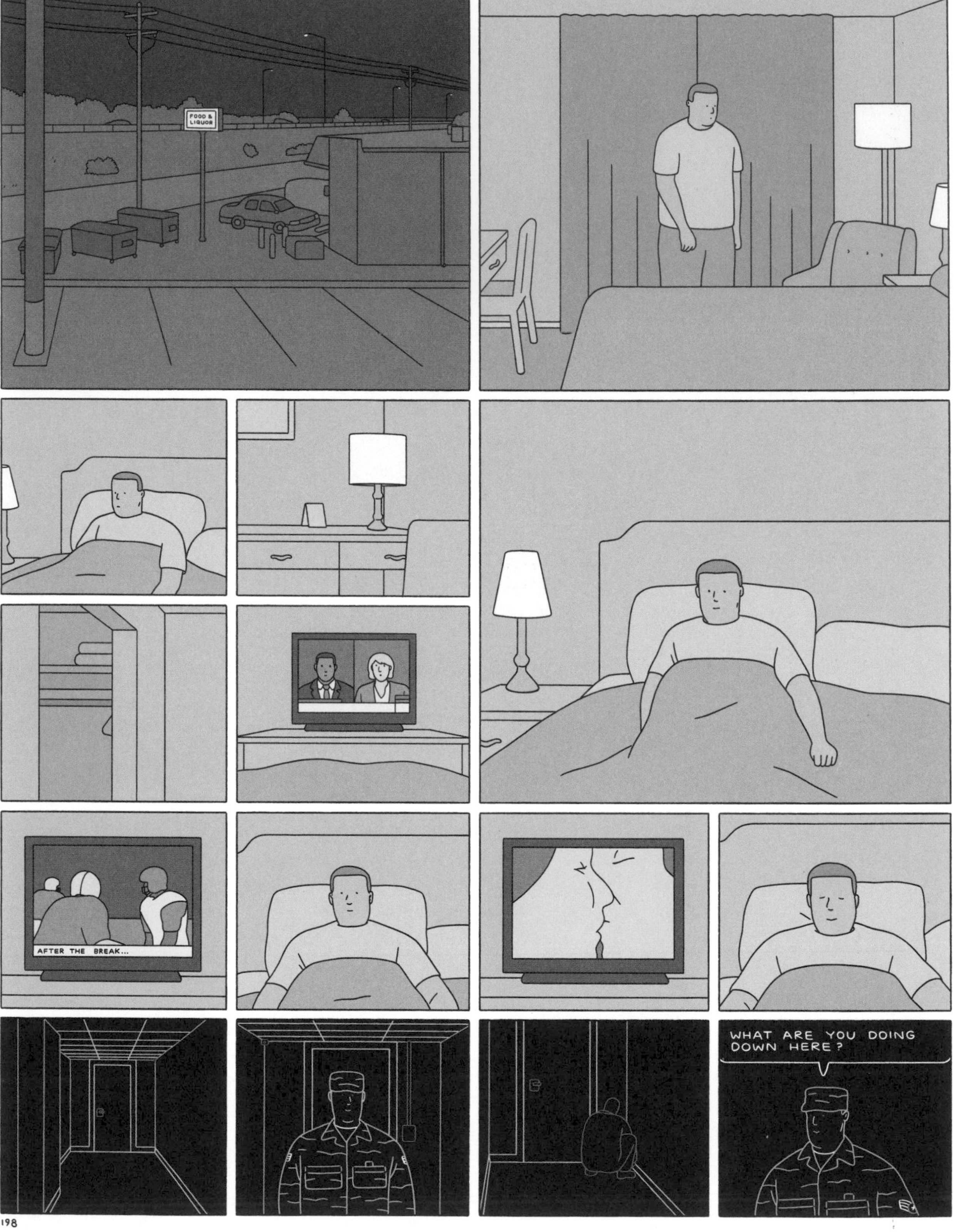
FOOD & LIQUOR
AFTER THE BREAK...
WHAT ARE YOU DOING DOWN HERE?

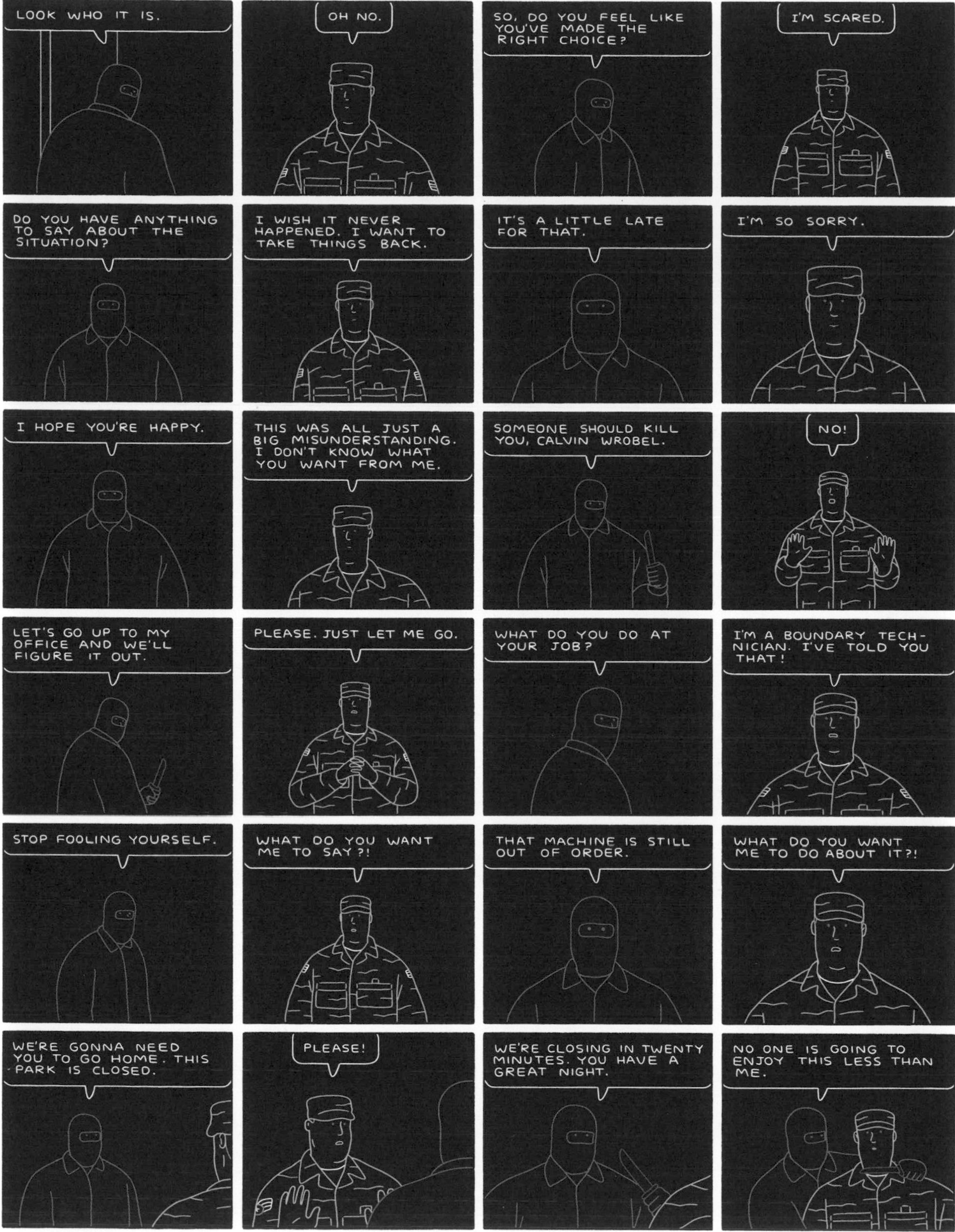
LOOK WHO IT IS.
OH NO.
SO, DO YOU FEEL LIKE YOU'VE MADE THE RIGHT CHOICE?
I'M SCARED.
DO YOU HAVE ANYTHING TO SAY ABOUT THE SITUATION?
I WISH IT NEVER HAPPENED. I WANT TO TAKE THINGS BACK.
IT'S A LITTLE LATE FOR THAT.
I'M SO SORRY.
I HOPE YOU'RE HAPPY.
THIS WAS ALL JUST A BIG MISUNDERSTANDING. I DON'T KNOW WHAT YOU WANT FROM ME.
SOMEONE SHOULD KILL YOU, CALVIN WROBEL.
NO!
LET'S GO UP TO MY OFFICE AND WE'LL FIGURE IT OUT.
PLEASE. JUST LET ME GO.
WHAT DO YOU DO AT YOUR JOB?
I'M A BOUNDARY TECH-NICIAN. I'VE TOLD YOU THAT!
STOP FOOLING YOURSELF.
WHAT DO YOU WANT ME TO SAY?!
THAT MACHINE IS STILL OUT OF ORDER.
WHAT DO YOU WANT ME TO DO ABOUT IT?!
WE'RE GONNA NEED YOU TO GO HOME. THIS PARK IS CLOSED.
PLEASE!
WE'RE CLOSING IN TWENTY MINUTES. YOU HAVE A GREAT NIGHT.
NO ONE IS GOING TO ENJOY THIS LESS THAN ME.

BANG
BANG

BANG
BANG

OPEN THE GOD. DAMN. DOOR!
BANG

SCOTT!

JESUS CHRIST, WOULD YOU SHUT UP?

THERE YOU ARE. IT'S ABOUT TIME!

SHUT UP. YOU'RE GONNA GET US KICKED OUT.

DON'T TELL ME WHAT TO DO. I'VE HAD IT!

GET OUT OF THE HALL-WAY. YOU'RE DRUNK. YOU'RE BEING AN ASSHOLE.

I'VE HAD ENOUGH OF THIS ANGER FROM YOU!

YOU SOUND LIKE A FUCKING IDIOT.

I'M NOT GONNA TAKE THAT!

THEN SIT OUT HERE AND THINK ABOUT WHAT YOU'VE DONE.

DON'T WALK AWAY FROM ME!

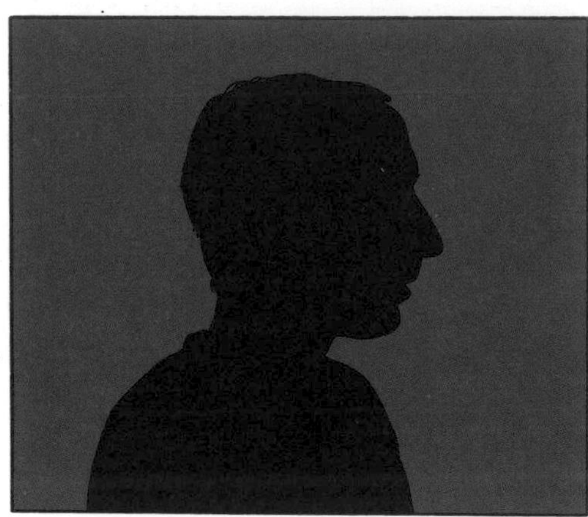

NICK DRNASO WAS BORN IN 1989 AND GREW UP IN PALOS HILLS, ILLINOIS. HIS FIRST BOOK, BEVERLY, RECEIVED THE LA TIMES BOOK PRIZE FOR BEST GRAPHIC NOVEL. HE LIVES IN CHICAGO WITH HIS WIFE AND THEIR THREE CATS.

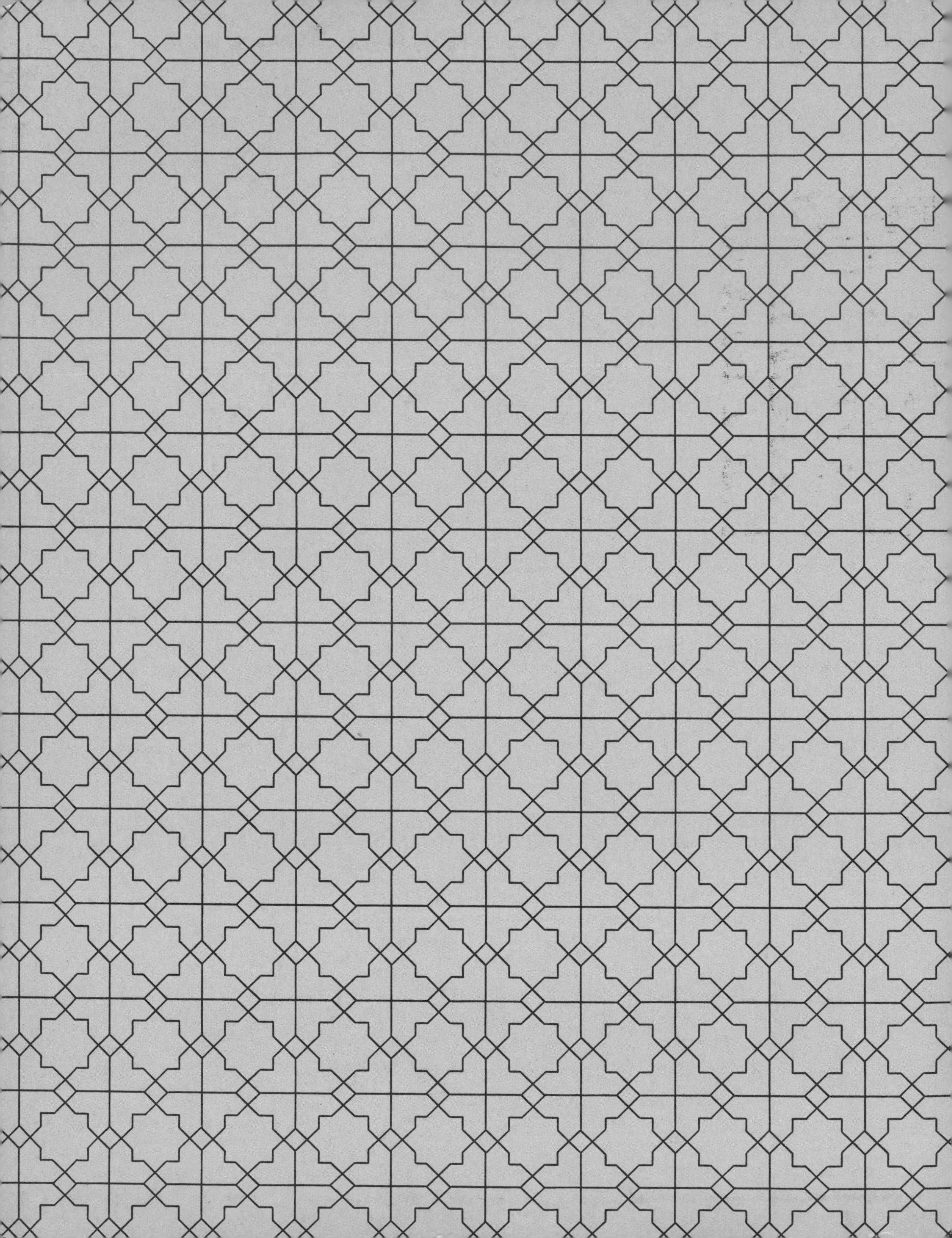